J. I. PACKER

His Life and Thought

ALISTER McGRATH

An imprint of InterVarsity Press
Downers Grove, Illinois

InterVarsity Press
P.O. Box 1400, Downers Grove, IL 60515-1426
ivpress.com
email@ivpress.com

*InterVarsity Press® is the book-publishing division of InterVarsity Christian Fellowship/USA®, a movement of
students and faculty active on campus at hundreds of universities, colleges, and schools of nursing in the United
States of America, and a member movement of the International Fellowship of Evangelical Students. For
information about local and regional activities, visit intervarsity.org.*

Cover design and image composite: David Fassett

ISBN 978-0-8308-4177-6 (print)
ISBN 978-0-8308-4178-3 (digital)

Library of Congress Cataloging-in-Publication Data
A catalog record for this book is available from the Library of Congress.

P 24 23 22 21 20 19 18 17 16 15 14 13 12 11 10 9 8 7 6 5 4 3 2 1
Y 41 40 39 38 37 36 35 34 33 32 31 30 29 28 27 26 25 24 23 22 21 20

Contents

Introduction

This short book is both a reflection on the life and an appreciation of the wisdom of James Innel Packer – 'Jim' to those who knew him well. It is not a standard biography, written for those who want to know the intricate details of Packer's career and the institutional politics which lay behind some of its turns. While the book draws on the wealth of material that I accumulated back in the early 1990s as I prepared to write the first major biography of Packer, it is primarily an exploration and appreciation of his legacy, investigating how the story of his life is interwoven with his vision of the Christian faith. As I discovered from extended conversations with Packer, he saw his life and faith as being intimately interconnected. I have learned much from knowing Packer and reading his works, and know others can benefit from his legacy as well.

I first came to appreciate the importance of Packer's story in November 1991, when I travelled from Oxford to Cambridge by coach to give a lecture. On boarding the bus, I discovered Packer was also a passenger. We had met in London two days earlier and sat down beside each other to continue our conversation as the coach wended its way through the English countryside on its long and slow journey to Cambridge. We had more than three hours together. Packer told me the story of his conversion at Oxford, and his gradual discernment of what he should be doing with his life. The story was so moving it led me to plan and write his biography over a period of five years, just as it has now led me to write this reflection on his life and thought. This book focuses on Packer's origins, education and ministry in the United Kingdom, which were an essential part of his formation as a Christian and as a theologian. Most of Packer's readers think of him as a North American theologian, having little appreciation of either his impact on evangelicalism in the United Kingdom, or the importance of the British context in shaping his outlook. Here I try to capture something of his British heritage, while nevertheless recognising that his greatest impact has been in North America. Although Packer was involved in numerous controversies throughout his career, he is valued today mainly for his positive contributions to the cultivation of a Christian mindset, and his constructive development of Christian spirituality.

C. S. Lewis regularly emphasised that great writers sought to share something with their readers – something which they themselves had grasped or seen and wanted to pass on to others, so that they might benefit. The best writers are not self-promoting narcissists who demand that we look *at them*, but those who invite us to look *through them* at what they have seen, enabling us to share in their experience. They are thus windows to something greater. Lewis himself saw authors not as spectacles to be admired, but as a 'set of spectacles' through which we can look at the world and see it in sharper focus and greater depth.

If Lewis is right, it follows that a good theologian should be transparent to the gospel. In other words, they avoid the cumbersomely technocratic language and obscurity of expression that prevents their readers from grasping what they have seen. In part, Packer's appeal lies both in his accessible and engaging writing style, alongside his seamless integration of a loving and attentive reading of the Bible, the weaving together of its themes in theology, and the working out of this vision of the Christian faith in holy living and prayerful adoration. In June 2016, Packer was asked what he hoped to achieve through his teaching for that year's Regent College summer school. His answer to that question deserves close attention.

> What I shall be saying to my class, in substance, is: Look! This is the biggest thing that ever was! And we Christians, most of us, still haven't appreciated its size. We've been Christians for years and years, and yet we haven't fully grasped it.

For Packer, theology is about unpacking this 'biggest thing that ever was' – faithfully and reliably. That is the evangelical core of preaching, prayer, proclamation and adoration. And it also stands at the heart of the joyful and prayerful discipleship of the mind that Packer calls 'theologising'.

Like the Puritans before him, Packer saw the natural place of the theologian as lying within the community of faith – not standing *above* the community of faith, still less standing *outside* it, but rather speaking to the Christian community as one who shared in their journey of faith and hoped to encourage them to reflect on it more rigorously and profoundly. This small volume aims to help its readers explore and reflect on what Packer so vividly describes as 'the biggest thing that ever was'. In retelling Packer's story, this book explores the interconnection of faith and life, opening up the ways in which the core ideas of Christianity change people as they become part of their lives.

For there is another point that needs to be made here. Theologians are not empty vessels containing abstract theological ideas, but are living souls who exhibit and embody those ideas and values in their lives. Packer embodies his theology by living out the central truths he discovered and sought to preserve and communicate. Our concern in this book is not primarily with documenting the details of Packer's life, but with the greater question of what he has seen, and what he wanted to pass on to others. Rather than summarise his career, and then reflect on the nature and importance of his ideas, I shall instead set the story of his life alongside reflection on the themes that were so important to him and remain significant to his many readers, allowing the vital interconnection of theology and life to be discerned.

Although I was an atheist as a teenager, I discovered the intellectual richness and deep spiritual wisdom of the Christian faith in 1971, during my first year as a student at Oxford University. I found myself struggling to grasp what Christianity was all about, and how I could live out this new way of seeing myself and the world in which I lived. I needed assistance from older and wiser Christians, who could help me sort out my ideas and what I was meant to be doing with my life. One of the writers I discovered in my first years of faith was C. S. Lewis. After reading a few of his books, I realised that he was a winsome writer with a grasp of the deep logic of

Christianity, who could help me grow in my own understanding. I still read Lewis with pleasure and profit to this day. He has become part of my personal story of faith.

In 1977, I discovered another writer who helped me consolidate my grasp of the Christian faith. As an undergraduate, I had heard Packer speak at some Christian meetings in Oxford in the early 1970s and, although I had found his ideas stimulating, I never managed to find the time to delve into his writing. Finally, I got round to reading one of Packer's books which was recommended by several of my friends – *Knowing God*. After half an hour, I knew I was in the presence of someone capable of writing eloquently and wisely about the Christian life, constantly making connections between the Bible, theology and personal spirituality. That book has become part of my personal story and remains one of the books to which I return, again and again. As I know from many conversations, countless others have also found Packer to be a source of wisdom and inspiration.

This short book cannot hope to be an adequate guide to either Packer's life or thought; it can, however, be a gateway for those who have yet to discover him, as well as for those who know something of him, and rightly sense that there is more to be uncovered, celebrated and remembered.

Alister McGrath
Oxford, July 2020.

I

The Beginnings of a Journey:
From Gloucester to Oxford

James Innell Packer was born in the English cathedral city of Gloucester on 22 July 1926, the son of James Percy Packer (died 1972), a clerk at the divisional headquarters of the Great Western Railway, and Dorothy Mary Harris (died 1965), who had trained as a schoolmistress in Bristol. Packer's sister Margaret was born in 1929 – the year of the Wall Street crash. The effects of this financial crisis on Britain were severe. By the end of 1930, unemployment in Britain had more than doubled from 1 million to 2.5 million. The Packer family, however, managed to cope with this austerity, living modestly in rented accommodation close to the city's railway station.

In September 1933, Packer began to attend the National School in London Road, Gloucester. He did not fit in easily with other boys at this junior school, and within days had become the victim of playground bullying. On 19 September, Packer was chased out of the school grounds onto the London Road – one of the busiest traffic thoroughfares in Gloucester. Perhaps the driver of a passing bread van was inattentive, preoccupied with his delivery schedules; more likely, however, he simply did not have time to react when a seven-year-old boy suddenly ran into his path. As a result of this collision, Packer suffered a major head injury. He was taken to the nearby Gloucester Royal Infirmary and rushed into an operating theatre.

Packer's condition was serious. He had suffered major damage to his skull on the right of his forehead, leading to injury to the frontal lobe of his brain. The resident surgeon at the hospital was able to extract fragments of bone from inside Packer's skull, leaving him with a small hole in his right forehead, some two centimetres in diameter. This injury would remain clearly visible for the rest of his life. After three weeks in hospital, Packer was allowed to return home, where he would spend six months recovering from the trauma of his injury. It was not until the spring of 1934 that he was allowed to return to the National School. Packer had to wear a protective aluminum plate over his injury, making it impossible for him to join in normal schoolboy games and sports.

During his period of convalescence away from school, Packer developed a love of reading which remained with him ever after. Packer's grandmother was an admirer of Agatha Christie and began to lend him some of her own books, including *The Mystery of the Blue Train* and *The Secret of Chimneys*. This appetite for books may have been a great asset for his later academic career, but at the time it probably reinforced the perception that he was a 'bookish' child who did not fit in easily with other children. Packer has freely admitted that he is 'something of a bookworm', devouring a wide range of literature that is reflected in many of his occasional pieces.[1]

After his return to the National School, Packer fell into the habit of accompanying his father on Saturdays when he returned to his office at Northgate Mansions, close to Gloucester Railway Station, to make sure the week's paperwork had been properly completed and filed. Packer later described his father to me as 'a railway clerk in charge of another clerk and two typists'. As a result, there were two typewriters in his father's office. His father used one of these to do his paperwork and, as nobody else was in the office on a Saturday afternoon, Packer was allowed to play around with the second. Noting how much their son enjoyed this typewriter, his parents gave him an old Oliver machine for his eleventh birthday in July 1937. Packer had secretly hoped to be given a bicycle, like all other boys of his age, but the risk of worsening his head injury through a fall made this impossible. He happily mastered the use of the typewriter and was soon typing out his own stories.

In September 1937, Packer left his local National School and moved on to the Crypt School in Greyfriars, Gloucester. The school had a long and distinguished history going back to 1539 and counted among its former pupils the great English preacher and evangelist George Whitefield (1714–70) and Robert Raikes (1736–1811), the founder of the Sunday School movement. On entering the school's sixth form, Packer chose to specialise in classics – the study of the language, literature and history of ancient Greece and Rome. He was the only pupil in his year who wished to take this option; as a result, he was taught on a one-to-one basis by the Headmaster of the school, David Gwynn Williams.

Williams is of considerable importance to our story, in that he became something of an intellectual role model to Packer. He had studied classics at Corpus Christi College, Oxford University. The close personal attention which he offered helped Packer to develop his own vision of what he wanted to do when he left the Crypt School. Like his Headmaster, he set his heart on going to Oxford University to study classics at Corpus Christi College. Williams' expert tuition helped Packer to build the competence and confidence that would be essential if he was to achieve this goal. Yet if Packer was to study at Oxford, this would require more than academic brilliance on his part; given his family's modest financial circumstances, he would need substantial scholarship support.

In March 1943, Corpus Christi College, Oxford, announced it would be awarding two major scholarships in classics for the following academic year: the Charles Oldham Scholarship, and the Hugh Oldham Scholarship. The scholarships, which would be awarded on the basis of a competitive examination to be held in Oxford on 7 September, were both worth £100 per annum, a very substantial sum at the time. Packer knew it was essential that he should win one of these scholarships; without this support, his family simply would not have been able to afford to send their only son to Oxford. Packer duly travelled to Oxford to sit the examinations, and shortly afterwards learned that he had been awarded the Hugh Oldham Scholarship – a remarkable achievement for someone who had only just turned seventeen.

Yet Packer's future at Oxford was still not certain. All able-bodied British males aged between eighteen and forty-one were liable to compulsory military service for the duration of the Second World War. If called up, Packer would have been able to begin his studies at Oxford that October but would have to interrupt them to serve in the armed forces when he turned eighteen. However, a medical examiner considered that Packer's head injury of 1933 exempted him from compulsory military service. That injury might have disqualified him from military service; it clearly did not impact on his intellectual capacities.

In the end, Packer decided he would defer entry to Oxford by a year. He would only have been seventeen in October 1943; it would, he concluded, be preferable to wait until he was eighteen and better prepared for the rigorous intellectual environment he knew he would experience there. This meant that he remained at the Crypt School. While everyone else in his year group left to go to college or take up jobs, Packer spent a third year in the sixth form, using the time and the school's library resources to read some of the classics of literature in preparation for his time at Oxford.

At this stage, Packer had little interest in Christianity, tending to regard it as probably true, but of little significance. Yet his interest was piqued by C. S. Lewis who, he later remarked, led him to 'something approaching orthodoxy'. He had read Lewis's *Out of the Silent Planet* in 1939 during a phase when he devoured stories about space-travel, and in his final years at the Crypt School read *The Screwtape Letters* along with the three smaller books that were later brought together to become the classic *Mere Christianity*.

Yet the young Packer remained puzzled by Christianity. Although he saw himself as doctrinally orthodox, something seemed to be missing from this rather cerebral account of the Christian faith. One of his schoolfriends tried to explain to him what it was all about. Eric Taylor had entered the sixth form at the Crypt School at the same time as Packer, and the two had struck up a friendship. While Packer stayed on at the school until the summer of 1944, Taylor had left a year earlier to study at the University of Bristol. During his first year at Bristol, Taylor was converted to Christianity through the ministry of the Bristol Inter-Faculty Christian Union. He wrote Packer a series of letters, in which he attempted to explain how he had discovered a living faith.

Packer found these letters somewhat baffling. He recalls his difficulty in understanding why Taylor believed that formal assent to the Christian creeds was not enough to mark someone as a Christian. What more could be required? The two friends met up in the summer of 1944, as Packer was preparing to go up to Oxford University. Despite Taylor's best efforts to describe the change that had taken place in his life, Packer was unable to comprehend it. In the end, Taylor suggested that Packer get in touch with the Oxford Inter-Collegiate Christian Union on his arrival and attend one of their meetings – a suggestion to which Packer agreed.

Oxford University: Studying Classics – Discovering Christianity

In the second week of October 1944, Packer left his parents to begin his life as an undergraduate at Corpus Christi College, Oxford. It was a momentous transition. Packer would be living away from his parental home for the first time, and entering an environment in which he had no friends or family. Oxford was a mere shadow of its normal self at that time since most able-bodied students and academic staff were serving in the armed forces. There were only a few eighteen-year-old students who would be studying for the regular three or four years for Oxford's undergraduate degree courses; most were undertaking truncated six-month courses before going on to undertake military service.

Like C. S. Lewis before him, Packer would study classical literature, history and philosophy. The two-part undergraduate course at Oxford which focused on these areas was popularly known as 'Mods' and 'Greats', although the University preferred it to be known as *Classical Moderations* and *Literae Humaniores*. While most of Oxford's undergraduate courses lasted three years, the intellectual rigour of classical studies required four. The demanding linguistic, philosophical and historical training which Packer would receive during his time at Oxford unquestionably lies behind his ability to handle complex arguments with ease and clarity. Though his Oxford tutors were excellent, Packer could not help but feel that they lacked the flair and pedagogical commitment of David Gwynn Williams. He had, he realised, been very fortunate in having had Williams as a mentor at such a formative stage in his life.

Shortly after his arrival, Packer was invited to attend a meeting of the Corpus Christi College Christian Union. This turned out to be a rather uninteresting affair. However, mindful of his promise to his

9

friend Eric Taylor, Packer subsequently agreed to go along to hear a
Christian Union sermon on the evening of Sunday, 22 October 1944
– 'Sunday of Second Week', to use the traditional Oxford way of
referring to days during a university term – at St Aldate's Church in
the centre of Oxford. The preacher, Earl Langston from the southern English coastal town of Weymouth, told his audience about his
own conversion, which had taken place at a Boys' Camp. He had
been asked by one of the older boys if he really was a Christian. This
unexpected challenge forced him to acknowledge that he was not,
and subsequently led him to make a personal response to Christ.

Packer had found the first part of the sermon a little dull, but this
narrative of conversion spoke to him deeply, appealing to his imagi-
nation. A picture took shape within his mind. He was looking
through a window into a room where some people were partying,
enjoying themselves by playing games. As he watched, he found he
could understand the rules of the games they were playing. But he
was *outside*, while they were *inside*. Packer recalled grasping his situation with crystalline clarity. *He needed to come in.*

The service ended with the singing of Charlotte Elliot's famous
hymn, 'Just as I am', with its constant emphasis on coming to Christ
– 'O Lamb of God, I come'. Packer made his decision: it was time
for him to come inside. And so, not far from the place where the
great evangelist George Whitefield committed himself to Christ in
1735, Packer made his own personal commitment.

Six weeks later, close to the end of his first term at Oxford, Packer
had a second experience which he often recounted in his later writings. Thirteen years earlier, C. S. Lewis had described a ride with a
friend to Whipsnade Zoo. At the start of this journey, he did not
believe that Jesus Christ was the Son of God; at the end, he did.
Lewis was not entirely clear how this radical change of mind
happened. It was as if a series of disconnected ideas suddenly fused
together, leading him to a compellingly clear conclusion. Packer
considers something very similar to have happened to him concerning his views on the Bible.

> In 1944 I went to a Bible study at which a vision from the book of
> Revelation (I forget which one) was expounded, and whereas at the

start I did not believe that all the Bible (which I had been assidu-
ously reading since my conversion six weeks before) is God's trustworthy instruction, at the end, slightly to my surprise, I found
myself unable to doubt that indeed it is . . . When, years later, I
found Calvin declaring that every Christian experiences the inward
witness of the Holy Spirit to the divine authority of Scripture, I
rejoiced to think that, without ever having heard a word on this
subject, I had long known exactly what Calvin was talking about.[2]

So was this some kind of experiential flash in the pan, an expression
of religious enthusiasm lacking any real intellectual substance? Not
in this case. Recognising his need to think through and consolidate
what he had experienced, Packer turned to George Whitefield as a
possible role model and mentor. After all, he had attended the same
school as Whitefield, and both had been converted in the same city
and university. Packer went to the city library and borrowed the two
volumes of an 1876 biography of Whitefield. They would be his
staple reading over the forthcoming Christmas vacation, which he
spent with his family in Gloucester. Packer found that studying
Whitefield was both enriching in itself, as well as serving as a gateway to the riches of the Reformed theological tradition.

Discovering the Importance of Theology

During the 1940s, the Oxford Inter-Collegiate Christian Union fell
under the influence of what is often described as the 'Keswick holiness teaching' or 'victorious living'. Although this teaching took
various forms, its central theme was that Christians come to a point
of crisis in their lives when they realise they cannot live victoriously
in their own strength. In this moment of crisis, God assures them
that they can surrender to Christ, trusting in his power to give them
victory over sin. The Keswick approach offered what many Christians
longed for: full deliverance from sin and a closer relationship with
Christ than anything that they had hitherto experienced. The slogan
that lay behind this understanding of how sin might be conquered
and expelled was simple: 'Let go, and let God'.

During 1945, Packer found himself deeply troubled by this teaching. Like many, he longed for the state of sustained victory over sin which the Keswick preachers so enthusiastically described, and in which Christians would be enabled to avoid failure and achieve things which were otherwise beyond them. Yet he found that his attempts at 'total consecration' seemed to leave him exactly where he was before – 'an immature and churned-up young man, painfully aware of himself, battling his daily way, as adolescents do, through manifold urges and surges of discontent and frustration'.[3]

His fellow students who followed the Keswick teaching urged him to figure out what barrier he was unwittingly placing in the path of the blessings that awaited him. He should surrender himself totally to the lordship of Christ, and experience the victorious presence of Christ within him. Yet, as Packer later reflected, the technique did not work – and could not work: 'Since the teaching declared that everything depends on consecration being total, the fault had to lie in me. So I must scrape my inside again to find whatever maggots of unconsecrated self-hood still lurked there.'[4]

Throughout this process of critical reflection, Packer never doubted that he was a Christian, nor did he have any concerns over the truth of the Christian faith. Both these matters were settled in his mind. The difficulty involved the tension he was experiencing between a specific (and influential) way of understanding the Christian life and his own experience of that life. Something was wrong. But what?

Packer clearly needed a theological framework within which he could position and understand his spiritual struggles – and thus find a solution to them. He was certain that the Keswick position was unsatisfactory. Yet recognising the failure of one approach does not in itself indicate what the best answer might be. In the end, Packer's answer came to him unexpectedly, when he was asked to curate a collection of old books that had been given to the Oxford Inter-Collegiate Christian Union by C. Owen Pickard-Cambridge, a former scholar of Balliol College, Oxford, who went on to serve as a missionary in Japan and later as Vice-Principal of the Bible Churchmen's College in Bristol.

The history of evangelicalism offers many instances of an apparently chance reading of Puritan classics leading to the personal spiritual revival of those who went on to become leading Christian preachers and evangelists. We might think of John Pawson (1737–1806), who relates how Joseph Alleine's *Alarm to the Unconverted* (1672) providentially fell into his hands – we are not told how! – and triggered the process of his conversion.⁵ Or William Grimshaw (1708–63), who accidentally came across a copy of John Owen's treatise on justification (1677) lying on a table in a friend's house – and, on opening the work and discovering its topic, felt 'an uncommon heat' flush his face.⁶ As one of his biographers put it, Grimshaw had realised 'he could not put himself right with God by a multitude of devotional exercises, however arduous'. Yet there seemed to him to be no way out of his dilemma – until he read John Owen.

Something very similar happened to Packer in Oxford's Northgate Hall in 1945. Packer's reputation as a somewhat bookish person led John Reynold, the Christian Union's Senior Librarian, to suggest that Packer might like to organise and catalogue the collection. As Packer worked through the piles of books, he came across a complete set of the writings of John Owen (1616–83), a noted Puritan preacher and theologian who had been appointed by Thomas Cromwell to be Vice-Chancellor of Oxford University during the period of the Puritan Commonwealth.

What attracted Packer's attention, however, was not Owen's close links with Oxford University, but the titles of two of Owen's treatises, which appeared to address and illuminate his own spiritual anxieties: 'On Indwelling Sin' and 'On the Mortification of Sin'. These works, he found, spoke directly to his condition. As he later recalled, 'Owen helped me to be realistic (that is, neither myopic nor despairing) about my continuing sinfulness and the discipline of self-suspicion and mortification to which, with all Christians, I am called.'⁷

Packer went on to write a synopsis of Owen's approach, which he circulated to other students in the hope that they might share his liberating experience – not, it has to be said, with any great success. However, his concise summary and application of Owen's insights laid the ground for his later and more systematic exploration of the relevance of the Puritan heritage for today. Here, he believed, was a theologically serious and pastorally rooted approach to the problems of the Christian life, which could be part of his emerging evangelical vision of faith. It was a theological epiphany which opened his eyes and his mind to a viable and defensible way of understanding and living out the life of faith. It has remained at the heart of Packer's spirituality and theology ever since.

So what did Packer discover in Owen? Put briefly, Packer realised that, despite being a regenerate believer, sin remained a presence within him. Sin was a self-serving energy in the fallen human spiritual system, which had to be constantly challenged and corrected by focusing on Christ. He would have to learn to be watchful for sin's presence and influence, and pray for strength to resist it. Packer's characteristic emphasis on what he later called 'disciplined, Bible-based, Spirit-led self-examination' flows out of his early reading of Owen.

Ministry: The Decision to be Ordained

Following the end of the Second World War in the summer of 1945, Packer gave long and careful thought to what he ought to be doing with his life. He might, of course, become a classics teacher, trying to do for others what David Gwynn Williams had done for him – imparting a vision for scholarship. Yet this did not seem right. He had a deep sense of wanting to serve God, and believed that this was best done through ministering within a church. He was not quite clear what specific form this ministry might take, but knew that he felt called to full-time ministry in some shape or form. While Packer was aware of his own personal limitations, he believed it was important to offer his talents, no matter how limited they might be, in the service of Christ. If God really wanted him to serve in this way, God would have to find a means of overcoming his weaknesses.

But within which church should he minister? Packer had attended the local Plymouth Brethren Church in east Oxford during his first two years as an undergraduate. It was a formative experience, and allowed him to benefit from its preaching, as well as the friendship of some older academic members of the congregation, especially James M. Houston and Donald Wiseman. From October 1946, though, Packer settled down as a member of the congregation of St Ebbe's, an evangelical Church of England parish in the centre of Oxford, which was experiencing new growth under the leadership of Maurice Wood. By the end of 1946, Packer had come to the conclusion that he ought to offer himself for ministry in the Church of England. Although he had misgivings about the Church of England itself, he believed that he would to be able to work – perhaps even to flourish – within its structures, which would allow him to deploy his talents where there were real needs.

Packer set out his reasons for being – and remaining – a member of the Church of England in a pamphlet he published thirty-five years later. He was not an Anglican on account of his personal history, but because he had come to consider it the best option for someone in his position, despite its faults and weaknesses. Why? Because of its rich theological and spiritual heritage.

> I am an Anglican not so much by sentiment or affection as by conviction . . . I cannot say that I ever particularly liked the Church of England as I found it, but I remain an Anglican out of conviction that here is the right place, for here I possess the truest, wisest and potentially richest heritage in all Christendom.[8]

Historically, Packer believed, the Church of England was given its identity, coherence and theological legitimacy by the creeds, the Thirty-Nine Articles (1563) and the Prayer Book (1662), set alongside a core commitment to the norms of Scripture, tradition and reason. This helps us understand Packer's concern during the 1960s with the theological consequences of the erosion or displacement of these historical boundary-markers, particularly the Thirty-Nine Articles.

Packer's decision to offer himself for ministry did not, of course, mean that he would automatically be admitted to the Church of England's theological education and ministerial formation programmes. He was invited to attend a 'Selection Conference' early in 1947, at which he was interviewed by a group of selectors to discern his motivation for offering himself for ministry, his pastoral gifts and his educational achievements. Typically, these conferences involved three days spent with other candidates and five selectors. The candidate would have private interviews with each of the selectors, after which they would confer and reach a joint decision on the ministerial potential of each of the candidates attending the conference. Within a week, Packer was told the outcome: he had been recommended for training for ministry in the Church of England.

The Church of England required its ordinands – those preparing for ordination – to study at one of a number of established 'theological colleges', and was generally happy for its students to choose the college at which they would train. Packer self-identified as an evangelical Anglican, with a strong emphasis on the importance of the Bible as a source of Christian doctrine and as a guide to Christian living. In 1947, there were four theological colleges in or near Oxford which were recognised as centres of ministerial education by the Church of England, one of which had an evangelical tradition. Packer already knew both the Principal and Vice-Principal of Wycliffe Hall through his church connections, and considered that it was an obvious home for him during his period of training for ministry. He felt he could flourish there.

We shall return to this narrative in Chapter 3. It is appropriate at this point, though, to reflect further on a theme introduced in this chapter, which has been of central importance to Packer throughout his whole career – the recognition that today's Christians can be enriched and informed through the wisdom of the past. Packer's discovery of the writings of John Owen proved to be a spiritual and theological gateway, opening his eyes and mind to the riches to be found there.

2

Old Books and Deep Wisdom: The Importance of the Christian Past

Packer's 1945 discovery of the personal spiritual value of the writings of John Owen clearly came as a surprise to him. Confronted with an inadequate twentieth-century response to an age-old problem, his initial instinct might have been to look around for another recent solution that seemed more palatable or workable. Yet Packer's accidental encounter with the Christian past helped him to acknowledge that most questions arising from Christian faith have been engaged with before. So might some of those classic responses remain helpful today, capable of guiding and informing our own thinking?

Packer certainly thought so. Back in the 1970s, when I was developing a research project that focused on theological writers of the Middle Ages, I came to know many of Oxford's medievalists, who kindly offered me advice and guidance as I began to research the field. Many of these scholars, I noticed, seemed to be more at home in the Middle Ages than in 1970s' Britain. To all intents and purposes, they found in their scholarship a means of escape from modern reality, allowing them to inhabit a more congenial parallel universe. I never felt like that in the late 1990s when I spent time with Packer in his Vancouver office. The bookshelves were filled with classic works of theology and spirituality, most dating from the seventeenth century; yet Packer saw these as a way of resourcing and enhancing his engagement with the questions and concerns of the 1990s.

Reading Owen as a student revealed to Packer the rich theological legacy of the past. Today's Christians can, he came to appreciate, learn from those who have made the journey of faith before us. C. S. Lewis made much the same discovery, and frequently wrote about the importance of the past to the life of faith and the tasks of theology. Perhaps his best discussion of the issue is found in Lewis's introductory preface to one of the most influential works of Christian theology, dating back to the fourth century – Athanasius of Alexandria's treatise on the incarnation. For Lewis, this represents a classic discussion of the theme, which transcends the barriers of culture and history. It has become a central reference point for contemporary discussion, precisely because it sets out the issues so well and incisively.

Lewis began to read Christian classics as a result of his interests in English literature, and soon realised that books become classics for a reason – namely, that people continue to find in them something of value and excellence, to which they return again and again. Classic writers help us to break free from our naive assumption that the most recent is the best, that somehow the wisdom of the past is discredited or eclipsed by more contemporary writing. More recent books are in the process of being assessed; some will stand the test of time, and others will not. The greatest challenge a book faces is perhaps not how it is judged today, but how it will be judged a generation from now. Will it be *valued*? Will it be *remembered* at all?

Christian classics – such as Athanasius' treatise *On the Incarnation* or Augustine's *Confessions* – possess the ability to tether us to our collective past, offering us resources that not only inform us about our faith but also reveal the blind spots of our own chronological parochialism. They anchor us to a continuous tradition of reflection, allowing us to see the great questions and problems of our own time and culture through the eyes of others. As Lewis observed in his own introduction to Athanasius' *On the Incarnation*, we need to 'keep the clean sea breeze of the centuries blowing through our minds, and this can be done only by reading old books'.[1] One of the chief values of old literature lies in its ability to challenge some of the assumptions that we take for granted as self-evidently correct, but which are actually culturally situated, and will one day seem strange to future generations.

Packer had great respect for Lewis, whom he saw as 'a fellow-Oxonian, a fellow-Greats man, and a fellow-Anglican, whose clarity of mental and moral insight, both as a human being and as a Christian, continues to astound me the more I read and re-read him'.[2] Like Lewis, although with his own distinct focus, Packer maintained and developed this strategy of critical appropriation and retrieval throughout his career, seeing himself as someone who garnered riches from the pasturelands of the past in order to make them available, intelligible and accessible to a new readership today. Here is how he described his own approach to theology in 1996:

> I theologize out of what I see as the authentic biblical and creedal mainstream of Christian identity, the confessional and liturgical 'great tradition' that the church on earth has characteristically maintained from the start.[3]

For Packer, 'keeping regular company with yesterday's great teachers' helps us to open our eyes to wisdom that might otherwise be denied to us.

As Packer rightly saw, this has important implications for how we approach historical theology. In studying the past, we can think of ourselves as stepping into the laboratory of faith, seeing how ideas were developed and explored, and checked out against their biblical moorings, their apologetic potential and their capacity to deepen our love for God – to mention just three criteria, to which more could be easily added.

This kind of respect for classics is not a form of antiquarianism, a nostalgia for a bygone age which values the past because it is old, or because it diverges so much from today's patterns of thought and value. Not every old book is a classic. What makes a book special is the quality of its vision of life, its capacity to help us grasp the grace of God and the love of Christ, or to challenge our own tendency to limit the gospel to what we can understand. And when we find such a book, we want to hold on to it, and share its wisdom and vision. That's why Packer typed out a twenty-page précis of Owen's arguments during his third year at Oxford. He wanted to capture Owen's vision of the Christian life and share it with others. 'Look what I have found! Does this help you as much as it has helped me?'

The profound theological heritage of the past can help us expand our vision of Christian truth by allowing us to see the gospel with a new awareness, and challenging our historical and cultural limitations. Lewis spoke of the capacity of literature to open our eyes to a richer vision of reality in a way that 'heals the wound, without undermining the privilege, of individuality'. ○K

> My own eyes are not enough for me, I will see through those of others . . . In reading great literature, I become a thousand men and yet remain myself. Like the night sky in the Greek poem, I see with a myriad eyes, but it is still I who see.[4]

Engaging with the wisdom of the past, Lewis suggests, enables us 'to see with other eyes, to imagine with other imaginations, to feel with other hearts, as well as our own'.[5] Packer transposed this general principle into a tool for the fresh appreciation and application of the Puritan legacy.

Now some will rightly raise a concern about Lewis's approach – and hence also with Packer's. Many will be sympathetic to their call to retrieve the legacies of the past, and allow these to enrich the life and thought of the present. Yet surely we need help here? How can we be certain that we have understood a past thinker, such as John Owen, for example? How can we work out which aspects of his thought can be applied to the present, and in what way? We clearly need an *interpreter* – someone who knows about Owen and can point us to the ways in which his ideas connect up with today's challenges and opportunities. This person needs to be rooted in both past and present in order to construct an interpretative bridge between the resources of the one and the needs of the other.

In what must be seen as a moment of theological discernment and vocational clarification, Packer realised that he could become such a bridge-builder, filtering, interpreting and applying the wisdom of the past to the issues of the present. As Packer explained to me in our conversations of the late 1990s, this was what he believed God might be calling him to do. One of the reasons that Packer wanted to enter ministry in the Church of England was to reinvigorate that ministry through rediscovering its historical roots in the thought of the European Reformation – especially Martin Luther and John Calvin – as well as the Puritan writers of the seventeenth century. Even as a student, Packer could see ways in which Owen and other thinkers of the past could enliven the ministry and preaching of today's churches.

He felt he was called to exercise such a ministry of retrieval and reappropriation.

Looking back over Packer's long career, it is now easy to see how this thread of thought is woven into most of his major publications. It is a central theme in the work for which he is best known – *Knowing God* (1973). At a more theological level, it plays an important part in Packer's development of the idea of the 'Great Tradition' in which past theological wisdom continues to nourish, inform and challenge today's churches, theologians and preachers. This does not entail believing that the old is necessarily the best, nor does it encourage a nostalgic retreat into the past; it is rather about allowing the past to challenge the present, in the expectation that this can only lead to the deepening and strengthening of the witness of the Church.

What theoretical frameworks, then, might help us understand this process of dialogue with the wisdom of the believing past? Up to about 1980, Packer seems to have developed his approach without drawing explicitly on any particular theory of interpretation. However, in 1980, a rising British evangelical scholar published a work exploring how the German philosopher Martin Heidegger's theory of the 'fusion of the horizons' of a past text and present inter-preter could help with the interpretation of the New Testament.[6] Anthony Thiselton's *The Two Horizons* was widely read and used by evangelicals; both John Stott and Packer told me how valuable they had found the work in stimulating their ministries. Stott found *The Two Horizons* helpful in avoiding 'the opposite pitfalls of unfaithful-ness and irrelevance, and be able to speak God's Word to God's world with effectiveness today'.[7] For Packer, the work helped him with his exegesis of the New Testament – but also offered an intellectual framework which affirmed the importance and legitimacy of what he was already doing with his notion of the 'Great Tradition'.

> What this means is that as the student questions the text he becomes aware that the text is also questioning him, showing him an alternative to what he took for granted, forcing him to rethink at fundamental levels and make fresh decisions as to how he will act henceforth, now that he has realized that some do, and he himself could, approach things differently.[8]

For Packer, studying the Christian past – as in, for example, the writings of John Owen – forces us to acknowledge that there are alternatives to what we take for granted, and that we could review the way in which we approach things. Packer's awareness of the enriching potential of the Christian past shaped his ideas about how best to teach theology – as we see, for instance, in his lectures at Regent College, Vancouver, during the 1980s and 1990s. Packer offers an excellent example of a 'theology of retrieval',[9] which provides important insights into how Christians today can reappropriate the past without being imprisoned by it.

To read Packer is to see these ideas in action. His inspiration for establishing the Puritan Studies Conference lay in his conviction that the Puritans had wrestled with some of the great questions of Christian living back in the seventeenth century – and that their concerns could easily be connected up with today's problems. His first book, *'Fundamentalism' and the Word of God* (1958), retrieved concepts developed by John Calvin in the sixteenth century and put them to use in the controversies of Packer's time, while his classic, *Knowing God* (1973), draws extensively on Calvin's ideas about what it means to 'know God', allowing them to penetrate and inform later Christian reflections on the life of faith. Historical texts, then, could play a vital part in fashioning today's Christian formation and, as we shall see (pp. 34–8), Packer developed a theological framework for ensuring that modern Christians could benefit from the deep wisdom of the Christian past without becoming trapped in a bygone era.

We must now resume our account of Packer's career, to understand how he began to think of himself as a theological educationalist, and then go on to achieve this goal.

3

Preparing for Ministry:
From Oxford to Birmingham

As the year 1948 opened, Packer's future seemed reasonably settled. He would graduate in June, at the end of the academic year, and then begin his theological studies at Wycliffe Hall in September in preparation for ministry in the Church of England. He was convinced of the need to take an Oxford degree in theology in order to be of maximum service in his future calling as a minister and preacher, and had managed to negotiate that he would be allowed to study theology as a second undergraduate degree through Corpus Christi College, while residing and being tutored at Wycliffe Hall.

Yet as the weeks progressed, Packer became less sure that this was the right way ahead. By the summer of 1948, he would have spent four years in Oxford. His studies at Wycliffe Hall would mean that he would spend a further two years in the same city and university. Might it not be wise to try and expand his horizons, to get away from Oxford for a year and do something different, before returning to take up his theological studies?

Wycliffe Hall was a 'theological college' of the Church of England – what North Americans call a 'seminary'. These colleges were not owned or managed by the Church of England; in effect, they were licensed or accredited by the Church to train people for ministry, and were inspected regularly to ensure that they met its professional and spiritual standards. There were other theological colleges with evangelical roots which were recognised in this way by the Church of England, such as Ridley Hall in Cambridge and Oak Hill College in Enfield, just north of London.

In the spring of 1948, Packer learned about an opening that had arisen at Oak Hill College for someone who could teach Latin and Greek for a period of twelve months. Packer's academic studies at

Oxford had required him to master both these ancient languages. He wrote immediately to Leslie Wilkinson, the Principal of Oak Hill College, expressing interest in the job and, after attending the College for an interview, was duly offered the position for a twelve-month period from September of that year, at a salary of £200, along with free board and lodging during College terms and vacations. Packer would be able to afford to stay at Oak Hill outside term, rather than having to return to his parents' home, as he had throughout his time at Oxford. He thus arranged to defer his studies at Wycliffe Hall by a year, and prepared himself enthusiastically, if slightly apprehensively, for his time at Oak Hill.

In the summer of 1948, Packer sat his final examinations in classics at Oxford University. He was widely expected to gain what Oxford calls a 'double first' (in other words, being awarded first class honours in both the first and second public examinations). In fact, he came very close to achieving this, gaining an outstanding second class degree. It was, however, a good enough academic performance to allow him to take the Final Honour School of Theology at Oxford after his return from teaching at Oak Hill College.

Oak Hill College, 1948–9

It is tempting to regard Packer's time at Oak Hill as a 'gap year' between studying classics and theology at Oxford. Yet this was to prove to be a transformational period for Packer's thinking about his future ministry in the Church and beyond. In my conversations with Packer during the 1990s, he mentioned several things that he gained from his time in Enfield.

First, and perhaps most importantly, he discovered his potential as a theological educator. 'I discovered', Packer told me, 'that nobody needed to teach me how to teach.' Although his main responsibility was to teach Latin and Greek to those students who needed them in order to meet the matriculation requirements of the University of London, he also ended up teaching his students how to engage with the Greek text of Ephesians, in preparation for the General Ordination Examination. He found it a deeply satisfying experience.

Some of his students from this period wrote to me, recalling his teaching skills with unanimous praise, as 'meticulous' and 'careful'. His slow and precise mode of speaking, which would probably be a disadvantage in social contexts, proved to be ideal when giving lectures.

As well as helping Packer gain a sense of confidence in himself, Oak Hill also opened his eyes to the importance of a specific form of ministry for which he seemed well adapted – theological education. In one sense, the Church of England at that time regarded all its clergy as potential theological educators – for example, in instructing those preparing for confirmation in the leading themes of the Christian faith, or through the communication of core gospel teachings through a regular preaching ministry. While Packer clearly valued these, he increasingly felt that his own calling might be to help equip those studying for ministry by providing them with a firm grasp of its theological foundations, and pointing them to outstanding exponents of its application – such as the Puritan writers he had come to value so highly.

But what could he do to prepare for this possibility, if it was indeed his true calling? Packer noticed that nobody teaching in British theological colleges seemed to have any significant research experience or even to have gained higher academic degrees, such as a PhD. The only exception he could think of was Geoffrey W. Bromiley, who was then a tutor in doctrine at the Bible Churchmen's Missionary Society College in Bristol (which would be renamed 'Tyndale Hall' in 1952), who subsequently went on to a distinguished teaching career at Fuller Theological Seminary in Pasadena, California. Bromiley had gained a PhD in 1943 from the University of Edinburgh with a dissertation on Johann Gottfried Herder and German Romanticism. He put his knowledge of German to good use later with a series of definitive translations of the works of leading German-speaking theologians, including some passages from Karl Barth's *Church Dogmatics*, as well as the whole of Wolfhart Pannenberg's three-volumed *Systematic Theology* and Helmut Thielicke's *Theological Ethics*.

As he reflected on his sense of calling to be a theological educator, Packer began to set himself some goals. To begin with, he would need to excel at Oxford in theology. It would not be enough to obtain an Oxford degree in theology; he needed to gain first class honours. He had nearly achieved this in classics; he would make it his aim to do so in theology. Yet this would not be an end in itself; it would be the gateway to what Packer now came to see as his most important goal – gaining an Oxford doctorate in theology, which could serve as the foundation for a career in theological education. This strong vocation to serve as a teacher would give Packer a pointed sense of direction and purpose when he returned to Oxford. A serious obstacle remained, however: given his family's very modest financial circumstances, Packer had no idea how he might be able to fund his research. He trusted that God would find a way for him to do this, if it was indeed his true calling.

Second, Packer established a new network of friends, some of whom (Alan Stibbs, for instance) would prove to be of major importance in encouraging his vocation and shaping his future career. One such friendship – consolidated rather than initiated during this period – was with Raymond Johnston, who had left Oxford in the summer of 1947. Johnson studied for a Diploma in Theology at London Bible College during the academic year 1947–8, and spent the next academic year at the University of London's Department of Education, in order to gain the qualification he needed to become a teacher of modern languages.

Both Packer and Johnston were working in or near London for the academic year 1948–9, and it was easy for them to meet up to hear Dr Martyn Lloyd-Jones preach at the Sunday evening service at Westminster Chapel, close to Buckingham Palace in central London. By then, Lloyd-Jones had established his reputation as one of England's finest Reformed preachers. This friendship would lead to the enactment of Packer's emerging vision of the retrieval of the wisdom of the past, initially through their joint publication in 1957 of an edition of Martin Luther's classic *Bondage of the Will*, and more significantly through the establishment of the Puritan Studies Conference – to which we shall return later (see pp. 34–8).

Wycliffe Hall, Oxford, 1949–52

In September 1949, Packer returned to Oxford to begin his theological studies at Wycliffe Hall. I began to write my biography of Packer shortly after I became Principal of Wycliffe Hall in 1995, and was delighted by the many letters I received from former students recalling their memories of Wycliffe and Packer nearly fifty years earlier. There were fifty-four students at Wycliffe during the year 1949–50, with the result that the Hall community was small enough for everyone to get to know each other. Students of the period remembered Packer well. He served as one of the editors of the Hall's student newspaper, and for a while was captain of the Wycliffe Hall table tennis team.[1] Although he was soon labelled a 'bookish' person, Packer had little difficulty in making friends within the College's student body.

One early friendship was with John Gwyn-Thomas, whom Packer met over their first evening meal together at Wycliffe Hall in September 1949. In the course of their conversation, Packer mentioned that he was a Puritan addict, and that he especially valued their thinking on mortification. 'Mortification!', Gwyn-Thomas responded, 'Let's have a talk after the meal.' The two students went on to spend two hours in the nearby University Parks, walking up and down the banks of the River Cherwell, discussing the theme of mortification and the inadequacy of popular notions of Christian perfectionism which failed to take the reality of sin seriously. The conversation confirmed Packer's estimation of the realism of the Puritan worldview, and his growing determination to develop and apply it further.

Packer's main aim was to achieve an excellent result in Oxford University's Final Honour School of Theology. As a graduate of Oxford, he would be entitled to complete the course in one year. Packer had planned this year carefully, making good use of his vacations while teaching at Oak Hill. He had already mastered the material for several of the examination papers before arriving at Wycliffe and threw himself into his studies for the remaining topics, such as patristics (the study of the theology of the early church) and the philosophy of religion. The academic preparation had paid off: Packer was awarded first class honours.

Sadly, Packer's family had no financial resources to pay for these studies. But to his delight, Packer learned that his performance in the theology examinations was so outstanding that the University awarded him a Liddon Theological Studentship (named after the noted nineteenth-century Oxford theologian H. P. Liddon) for two years. He was also awarded a Local Education Authority grant from his home town of Gloucester. Taken together, these two awards provided Packer with enough funds to enable him to do research for an Oxford doctorate. Moreover, other than meeting a real financial need, these awards also served a deeper purpose for Packer: they confirmed his vocational sense that this research was what he was *meant* to be doing, just as his time at Oak Hill had solidified his awareness that his future might lie in a ministry focusing on theological education. As Packer often remarked to me in our conversations, it was as if his sense of calling was gradually being confirmed and consolidated.

There was never any doubt in Packer's mind about the topic he would research for his Oxford doctorate. His growing interest in the Puritan heritage had led him to focus on the theology of salvation of Richard Baxter (1615–91). Packer set himself the task of providing 'a full, sympathetic exposition of Richard Baxter's doctrine of man, created and fallen; of his redemption by Jesus Christ; and of the restoration in him of the image of God through the obedience of faith by the power of the Holy Spirit'. The topic was interesting for several reasons, not least because of the significant divergences between Baxter and John Owen in this area (Puritanism, it must be appreciated, was more theologically diverse than is sometimes assumed). The Faculty of Theology confirmed it was willing for him to carry out this research on Baxter for his thesis and appointed Geoffrey Nuttall, the author of the highly acclaimed work *The Holy Spirit in Puritan Faith and Experience* (1946), as his supervisor.

Everything seemed to be falling into place, confirming Packer's intuition that his future lay in theological education. That crystallising conviction was reinforced by an invitation to teach biblical theology and philosophy of religion to thirty women students at St Michael's House, a few minutes' walk from Wycliffe Hall. In July 1952, Packer's first published article on 'The Puritan Treatment of

Justification by Faith' *Alone* appeared in *The Evangelical Quarterly*.[2] Furthermore, his research was going well, and by the time he left Wycliffe Hall in December 1952, he felt he had enough material to begin writing up his thesis for examination.

Packer's admiration of the theological legacy of the Puritans found expression in another way. He had maintained his friendship with Raymond Johnston and Martyn Lloyd-Jones since leaving Oak Hill, and now put this to good use. In addition to undertaking original research on Baxter, one of the most important Puritan writers, Packer teamed up with Johnston to organise a 'Puritan Studies Conference', to be held annually at Westminster Chapel in London, with Lloyd-Jones as the keynote speaker. The first such conference in December 1950 attracted twenty people, mostly students. By the middle of the 1950s, numbers had increased to sixty; by the end of the 1950s, to more than a hundred.

It was a remarkable achievement, providing a serious forum for discussion of Puritan theological principles and their application, with constant reference to the needs of the churches today. The 'Banner of Truth Trust' was founded by Iain Murray, Sidney Norton and Jack Cullum in July 1957, with the objective of reprinting the classic works of Puritan theology to meet the growing appetite for these works created by the Puritan Studies Conference. Packer's initiative generated changes in the perception of Puritanism within British evangelicalism. What was once seen as a marginal and slightly arcane interest came to be regarded as having potential to enrich mainstream evangelical reflection.

The Move to Birmingham: Ministry and Marriage

Packer had not, however, given up on the idea of ordination in the Church of England. His vision of becoming a theological educator was firmly linked to his ministry in that same church, which would allow him to make connections between the riches of Christian theology (especially those he found in the writings of the Puritans) and the life and practice of faith. But where would he minister? Packer was naturally attracted to London, and had a particular regard for All Souls, Langham Place, which was then emerging as a leading centre of evangelical thought under the ministry of John Stott. In the end, however, nothing came of this. A possibility also opened up in Cheltenham, one of the major towns in Packer's home county of Gloucestershire. Again, this came to nothing.

Packer's breakthrough arrived through a chance conversation with Alan Stibbs, one of the friends he had made during his time at Oak Hill College. Stibbs mentioned that he had heard that William Leathem was looking for a curate to join him in his ministry in Harborne, a suburb of England's second city, Birmingham. Leathem was an active evangelical, with particular links with the Bible Churchmen's Missionary Society, and a strong sense of the importance of the local church in preaching and spiritual growth. Packer went to visit Leathem in Birmingham in the autumn of 1952, and decided immediately that this was an environment in which he could minister. Leathem concurred and offered Packer the position of curate of the parish of St John's, Harborne, on an annual salary of £325 for a period of three years. After a formal interview with the Bishop of Birmingham, it was agreed that Packer would be ordained on 21 December 1952. He would live with William and Enid Leathem and their family in the vicarage, which had a spare room.

This arrangement suited Packer well. His pastoral and administrative duties were not arduous, and he found that he had time to get on with writing up his doctoral thesis, which was due for submission to the examiners by the second week of July 1954. Developments in Packer's personal life, however, meant that some changes would have to be made to his accommodation. He had met Kit Mullett, a Welsh trainee nurse, in the late spring of 1952 when he was speaking at a house party for Christian medical staff from St Bartholomew's Hospital, London. Kit was an admirer of Martyn Lloyd-Jones and regularly attended Westminster Chapel. Packer proposed to her during the Puritan Studies Conference at Westminster Chapel in December 1952. In the summer of 1953, Kit completed her qualifications as a nurse and obtained a position as a staff nurse at St Chad's Hospital, Hagley Road, only two miles away from Harborne.

Packer found himself stretched throughout the month of June 1954. Not only did he have to make arrangements for his wedding;

he also had to complete his Oxford doctoral thesis. William Leathem generously gave him some time off in June to allow him to complete his thesis on time. Happily, Packer managed to travel to Oxford and hand in three typewritten copies of the thesis in July only three days before the University deadline, in the same week as his marriage to Kit on 17 July 1954 in the local Memorial Hall, which was then still acting as a temporary church for St John's, Harborne. William Leathem conducted the service and Packer's friend Alan Stibbs preached.

Oxford's Faculty of Theology appointed two examiners for the thesis: Dr John Marsh (Principal of Mansfield College, Oxford) and R. L. Child (Principal of Regent's Park College, Oxford). The *viva voce* examination was set for 1 December 1954 at 2.00 p.m. at Regent's Park College. The outcome of the examination was not entirely surprising: in 1995 Geoffrey Nuttall, Packer's supervisor, told me that Packer's thesis was one of the best he had ever supervised or examined. The two Oxford examiners clearly took a similar view, and reported that the thesis was of such merit that Packer should unconditionally be awarded an Oxford DPhil (Oxford University has always used this abbreviation, where most other universities use PhD). Packer's goal of becoming a theological educationalist was now within reach; but what theological institution might offer him a teaching position?

Packer's vision was not to become an academic theologian, lecturing to university students who had no interest in Christian ministry. Rather, he saw himself as called to serve and resource those who would be preachers and pastors, giving them a solid theological foundation on which they could build their ministries. This meant that his most appropriate base would be one of the evangelical theological colleges of the Church of England, such as Wycliffe Hall or Oak Hill College. Yet neither had any teaching positions vacant in 1954.

Then news reached William Leathem that Tyndale Hall, Bristol, needed a new Tutor in Doctrine to replace Geoffrey Bromiley, who had accepted the position of Rector of St Thomas' Church, Corstorphine, just west of Edinburgh city centre. Leathem had no doubts about whom Tyndale's next Tutor in Doctrine should be.

Theological Education: The Move to Bristol

In November 1925, the Bible Churchmen's Missionary Society (BCMS) established a training college in Clifton, Bristol, to prepare ordinands for ministry in England or overseas. Initially known as the Bible Missionary Training College, it was renamed Tyndale Hall in 1952.[3] The Church of England recognised the Bible Missionary Training College as one of its theological colleges in 1927.

We noted earlier how Packer saw Geoffrey W. Bromiley as something of a role model for his own academic ministry on account of his obvious commitment to theological education and pastoral work, and the fact that he was a serious scholar with a PhD. At this time, it was most exceptional for those teaching in theological colleges to have such advanced qualifications; tutors were generally enthusiastic amateurs, tending to have educational interests rather than expertise, who would serve between three and five years in theological colleges before returning to parish ministry, which was where they felt they really belonged. Bromiley had served as Tutor in Doctrine at Tyndale since 1946, and his departure left a significant gap in the College's teaching capacity.

In those days, it was very unusual for theological colleges to advertise vacancies publicly. News of openings was generally shared through personal or institutional networks, in the hope that suitable candidates could be identified and then approached about the possibility of taking up the vacant position. Tyndale Hall's close links with the BCMS ensured that news of the vacancy arising from Bromiley's departure was circulated to its supporters – among whom was William Leathem, one of the most active networkers of the Society.

Leathem had little doubt that Packer was the ideal successor to Bromiley. Others within the BCMS clearly shared his view. There was, however, a difficulty, in that there existed a firm understanding within the Diocese of Birmingham that curates would serve two full years in their first post before being allowed to move on to something new. In effect, this meant that the earliest that Packer could take up the position of tutor at Tyndale Hall would be January 1955. Tyndale, however, wanted their new tutor in place by September 1954, to be able to teach from the beginning of the academic year 1954−5. It seemed a regrettable impasse had been reached.

But Leathem excelled in his ability to improvise. He could see an obvious way of getting round what he clearly regarded as nothing more than an irritating technicality. Leathem's workaround was simple: Packer would remain employed as his curate until the end of December 1954, while at the same time serving as a part-time visiting lecturer at Tyndale Hall from September of that year. After that, Packer and Kit would be able to move to Bristol permanently. Packer thus continued his ministry in Birmingham until the end of 1954, while spending the best part of two days a week teaching at Tyndale. He would take the first train from Birmingham to Bristol in the morning, and stay overnight at Tyndale, returning late the following day. It was not ideal, but enabled Packer to immerse himself partially in the teaching programme and College culture at Tyndale Hall.

Kit and Packer finally left Birmingham and moved to Bristol on a cold winter day in the first week of January 1955. Not owning a car, they travelled down to Bristol through sleet and snow in the van which was transporting their personal effects and furniture to their new home in the grounds of Tyndale Hall. They would live in a first-floor apartment in the main College building, located above the chapel and lecture rooms, and underneath student accommodation for half a dozen students.

As 1955 began, Packer found himself beginning to live out the vision that he had nurtured over the previous eight years. He had gained a first class degree and a doctorate in theology from Oxford University and was poised to begin his career as a theological educator. He now had more time to focus on one of his core concerns – how Puritanism might inform and enrich the ministry and preaching of the Church in the present day.

Given its immense importance for Packer, it is worth pausing here to explore in rather more detail the key role that came to be occupied in his thought by the Puritan theological and literary heritage.

4

Learning from History:
Retrieving the Puritan Heritage

As a gifted preacher, Martyn Lloyd-Jones found it easy to express deep truths in memorable ways. His pithy summary of the role of the annual Puritan and Reformed Studies Conferences at Westminster Chapel is an excellent example:

> It is always essential for us to supplement our reading of theology with the reading of church history . . . if we do not, we shall be in danger of becoming abstract, theoretical, and academic in our view of truth, and failing to relate it to the practicalities of life and daily living.[1]

The conferences are now seen as having played a significant part in reinvigorating evangelicalism across denominations in Great Britain, particularly within the Church of England during the 1950s and 1960s.

So why did Packer prize the Puritans so highly? And what did he think that his own generation of pastor-theologians might learn from them? We have already seen the theological framework within which Packer positions the Puritans: the fundamental belief that the wisdom of the past can be reappropriated by today's Christians, allowing it both to enrich and to challenge our own ideas and lives. In his writings, Packer not only developed this general principle, but at the same time applied it in the case of one specific body of wisdom and expertise which he believed to have particular relevance – the Puritan heritage.

Historians point out that 'Puritanism' is not an easy concept to define. Like the modern term 'evangelical', it designates such a wide range of theological opinions and institutional commitments that it is sometimes unclear whether it continues to be meaningful. The term 'Puritan' originated in England during the later sixteenth century, and was intended as a criticism, even a caricature, of a religious movement that seemed to threaten the Church establishment of the day. As Packer himself noted, 'Puritanism' was always 'a satirical smear word implying peevishness, censoriousness, conceit, and a measure of hypocrisy, over and above its basic implication of religiously motivated discontent with what was seen as Elizabeth's Laodicean and compromising Church of England.'[2] Some historians suggest that Puritanism was a form of English Protestantism that was characterised by its enthusiasm or zeal, rather than by its specific theological beliefs; others point out that it is impossible to avoid the conclusion that some central theological convictions – such as a strong doctrine of election – were integral to Puritan self-understanding.

At points, Packer speaks of the Puritans as being 'theologically homogeneous'.[3] Historians will find this statement problematic, given – to mention only one particularly obvious point – the very significant differences between Richard Baxter and John Owen on the doctrine of justification by faith, noted in Packer's doctoral thesis. Yet Packer's concern is primarily to learn from those who are broadly known as 'Puritans', whose characteristic 'mind-set' consisted in a rigorous biblical commitment to doctrinal and ethical precision, aiming at holiness of life.[4] Packer perhaps understates some of the theological differences that existed between leading Puritans on matters such as their understanding of the Church – but this is not of critical importance to his agenda, which is to enable us to learn from this body of wisdom from the past.

Packer's interpretation of the ongoing relevance and value Puritanism held for contemporary Christian living was set out in his landmark work *A Quest for Godliness: The Puritan Vision of the Christian Life* (1990). This important and influential work takes the form of a collection of papers, including nine lectures from the original Puritan and Reformed Studies Conferences, concerned both to delineate the Puritan vision of the Christian life and to embed this in today's Church. It allows a broad understanding of the theological, pastoral and spiritual vision of the Puritans which does not require

[handwritten margin note:] ✗ ALONE SOLA Fide'

35

agreement on what lies at the core of Puritanism, the precise extent of a 'Puritan era' or whether Puritans were – or ought to be – X Presbyterian, Anglican or Congregationalist. *Lutheran or METHODIST*

Packer locates the essence of Puritanism as lying primarily in its understanding of the transformation of humanity leading to spiritual 'maturity' – an amalgam of wisdom, goodwill, resilience and creativity. It was at heart 'a spiritual movement, passionately concerned with God and godliness'.[5] Although this vision was rigorously grounded in theology, it was essentially an experiential (or, to use the language of that age, an *experimental*) religion: 'Puritanism was essentially an experimental faith, a religion of "heart-work", a sustained practice of seeking the face of God, in a way that our own Christianity too often is not.'[6]

This aspect of Puritan theology needs to be emphasised, in that it avoids the somewhat dry and dusty approaches that treat theology as essentially abstract theorising about God. The American Presbyterian writer James Henley Thornwell was well aware of the inadequacy of an excessively rationalist or cerebral approach to theology, which failed to engage with human experience and emotion.

> It gave no scope to the play of Christian feeling; it never turned aside to reverence, to worship, or to adore. It exhibited truth, nakedly and baldly, in its objective reality, without any reference to the subjective conditions which, under the influence of the Spirit, that truth was calculated to produce. It was a dry digest of theses and propositions – perfect in form, but as cold and lifeless as a skeleton.[7]

Such an approach to theology divorces it from the realm of experience – and hence from the reality of everyday Christian life, especially among believers who did not find intellectual analysis natural or easy. Packer was clear that Puritanism avoided this unhelpful imbalance between reason, emotion and experience, and thus provided an important model of how theology should be done – a point to which we shall return when considering Packer's understanding of the relation of theology and spirituality (see pp. 101–12).

We have already seen how Packer's reading of John Owen's

X *or BAPTIST or PENTECOSTAL or GREEK ORTHODOX*

'Mortification of Sin in Believers' persuaded him that Puritanism offered a realistic and rigorous approach to sin, which was thoroughly rooted in the Bible. 'Without Owen,' Packer once remarked, 'I might well have gone off my head or got bogged down in mystical fanaticism.'[8] Owen's treatise can be read as an extended commentary on Romans 8:13: 'For if ye live after the flesh, ye shall die: but if ye through the Spirit do mortify the deeds of the body, ye shall live.' The word 'mortify' in the King James translation familiar to Owen and his contemporaries means 'to put to death'. Owen himself summed up the message of his treatise like this: 'Be killing sin or it will be killing you.'[9]

Packer's own spirituality – expressed in writings such as *Knowing God* – echoes some of the themes that he finds in the Puritans. As he later reflected, the Puritans 'made me aware that all theology is also spirituality, in the sense that it has an influence, good or bad, positive or negative, on its recipients' relationship or lack of relationship with God'.[10] Although Puritan spirituality is sometimes portrayed by its critics as other-worldly, inattentive to the problems and concerns of everyday life, Packer points out that this judgement is somewhat hasty and unperceptive: 'The Puritans' awareness that in the midst of life we are in death, just one step from eternity, gave them a deep seriousness, calm yet passionate, with regard to the business of living.'[11] While proclaiming that we should have heaven 'in our eye' throughout our earthly pilgrimage, they insisted that this 'hope of glory' must both inform and sustain our earthly life, affecting our relationships with others and our attitudes to the world around us. They viewed this life as 'the gymnasium and dressing room where we are prepared for heaven', teaching us that preparation for death is the first step in learning truly to live.[12]

Packer hoped that *A Quest for Godliness* would encourage readers in 'opening the windows of our souls to let in a breath of fresh air from the seventeenth century'.[13] It is a helpful image, drawing on C. S. Lewis's famous essay 'On the Reading of Old Books'. Opening a window allows fresh air to enter, both blowing away cobwebs and enabling us to breathe more easily. The image neatly conveys two central ideas: removing what is dead, useless or unhelpful, and renewing and revitalising our spiritual lives.

Packer's vision for the transforming, reforming and enriching impact of Puritanism on evangelicalism proved highly attractive to many evangelicals, particularly those concerned about the historical shallowness and theological superficiality of the movement. Packer's agenda helped catalyse increasing scholarly interest in Puritanism in both its British and North American forms, as well as a growing demand for Puritan writings which resulted in the publication of new editions of classic works and collections.

A further outcome of this fresh interest in Puritanism is the emergence of theological and devotional works which represent modern interpretations and applications of the Puritan heritage. An excellent example is found in John Piper's outstanding work *Desiring God*, which sets out some of the leading themes of the spirituality of Jonathan Edwards, perhaps the greatest American Puritan writer.[14] Although Piper began to read Edwards while a student at Fuller Theological Seminary, he only appreciated his full significance when working on his PhD at the University of Munich, when he began to appreciate Edwards' remarkable ability to illuminate and inform contemporary concerns and issues.[15] For both writers, wise *retrieval* of the past leads to individual and communal *renewal* in the present.

Packer built up a significant library of Puritan classics over the years, partly to resource his own research and teaching, but also for his personal enjoyment. In 2002, Packer donated his collection of early printed books to Regent College's Allison Library. This collection of seventeenth-century Puritan literature includes John Bunyan's *Grace Abounding to the Chief of Sinners* (1692); many of Richard Sibbes' sermons printed in the 1630s and 1640s; a first edition of the *Works of William Perkins* (1613); and a first edition of Joseph Symonds' *Case and Cure of a Deserted Soule* (1639). These have now been digitised, and are freely available to scholars working in this field.

In the next chapter, we resume our main narrative, following the Packers as they moved to Bristol, in England's west country.

5

The Theological Educationalist:
Tyndale Hall, Bristol

Bristol, a port city on the River Avon, is the most important population centre in England's west country. Its port played an important role in developing trade between England and North America. The slave trade brought prosperity to the city, but at a high moral price. The city's fortunes were given a further boost in the 1830s, when Isambard Kingdom Brunel developed the Great Western Railway, allowing direct travel between London and Bristol. The origins of higher education in the city can be traced back to the establishment of University College, Bristol, in 1876, which later became the University of Bristol in 1909.

The origins of Bristol Baptist College, the oldest institute of theological education in the city, can be traced back to the early eighteenth century. Methodism had significant roots in the region, following John Wesley's preaching ministry in the city during the great Evangelical Revival of the eighteenth century. After the Second World War Wesley College, Bristol, was founded to prepare students for ministry in the Methodist Church. Yet despite its regional importance, the Church of England had no centres of theological education in the area until the 1920s.

By the 1930s, however, Bristol had gained three Anglican institutions of theological training, all linked with the Bible Churchmen's Missionary Society (BCMS). The first to be established was the Bible Missionary Training College in 1925. In 1930, the BCMS established a second training college for women nearby, named Dalton House. In 1932, a serious disagreement arose between the Principal of the Bible Missionary Training College and the BCMS, which led to the Principal and his staff leaving and founding their own rival training establishment, to be known as 'Clifton Theological

College'. While there were initially fears that this would reduce the numbers of students enrolling at the Bible Missionary Training College, these proved unfounded. All three colleges remained viable after the Second World War, each having developed its own distinct identity.

Some prominent evangelical theological colleges in the Church of England were named after English Reformers – such as Wycliffe Hall, Oxford (named after John Wycliffe, the 'morning star of the Reformation') and Ridley Hall, Cambridge (named after Nicholas Ridley, a Protestant bishop martyred under Mary Tudor in 1555). In 1952, the Bible Missionary Training College decided to follow suit. It changed its name to 'Tyndale Hall', after the English Protestant Bible translator William Tyndale, who was martyred in Antwerp in 1536. This helped to highlight both the College's connections with the west of England, where Tyndale had been born, and its commitment to biblical studies.

In January 1955, following a period of four months as a visiting lecturer, Packer finally joined the staff team at Tyndale Hall as its full-time residentiary Tutor in Christian Doctrine. There were only two other residentiary members of staff at this time: the Principal, J. Stafford Wright, who specialised in the Old Testament, and the Vice-Principal, John Wenham, noted for his clear teaching of New Testament Greek. Wenham's textbook on this subject, published in 1966 by Cambridge University Press, became the standard text in England for a generation of theologians and ordinands. It was a relatively new staff team. Stafford Wright had only served as Principal since 1951, having previously been Senior Tutor at Oak Hill College from 1945 to 1950. Wenham was also a recent arrival, after serving as Vicar of St Nicholas' Church, Durham, from 1948 to 1953.

Most of the students at Tyndale Hall at this time were Church of England ordination candidates, who would go on to ministries in the national Church after leaving the College. As Tyndale Hall was not accredited to award its own degrees, the College registered its students for recognised theological qualifications offered by other academic institutions, most notably the University of Bristol's Bachelor of Arts in Theology, the University of London's Bachelor of Divinity and the University of London's Diploma in Theology.

All the College's ordinands were registered for the General Ordination Examination (GOE), which was the recognised professional qualification for ministry in the Church of England at this time. Tyndale Hall generally had a student body of about fifty-five to sixty during most of the period when Packer was on the teaching staff.

So what subjects did Packer teach? His main commitments were to teach early church history, the history and theology of the Reformation, biblical theology and a general doctrine course. One early outcome of this focus on the Reformation was the collaboration between Packer and Raymond Johnston to produce a new translation of Martin Luther's 1525 reforming treatise *The Bondage of the Will*. This translation, which was published in January 1957, included a substantial theological introduction stressing the ways in which contemporary evangelicalism seemed to have lost track of many of the insights of the Reformation.

But perhaps Packer's most significant contribution in his first period at Tyndale Hall was a critical review he published in 1955 in the *Evangelical Quarterly* of Steven Barabas's *So Great Salvation*, a work promoting the Keswick holiness teaching of that period.[1] As we noted earlier (see p. 11), Packer had come to the view that this rested on a theologically deficient understanding of our ability to make the critical decisions necessary to our sanctification. For Packer, we need good theology if we are to avoid the kind of loose thinking that arises from uncritical personal piety. His one-liner in that review stands out for its clarity and concision: 'Pelagianism is the natural heresy of zealous Christians who are not interested in theology.'[2]

What exactly did Packer mean by speaking of 'Pelagianism' in this way? The reference is to a debate which broke out in the Western Church in the early fifth century over a number of issues relating to grace and freedom – including the natural abilities of human beings to break free from the power of sin. The Keswick holiness teaching rested, in Packer's estimation, on an incorrect and potentially misleading understanding of the ability of fallen human nature to remedy its own situation. We have no natural ability to discern and choose what God wants; only the grace of regeneration can free us from this bondage to sin. Holiness is not a human achievement, no matter how much it may demand human effort. It is a work, an achievement, of the Holy Spirit, who informs, prompts and energises our efforts.

Packer's brutally incisive review alienated some and irritated others, mostly within the 'Old Guard' of British evangelicalism – including some older supporters of Tyndale Hall, who threatened to withdraw their support for the institution as a result of Packer's criticisms. Nothing, however, seems to have come of these threats. Many younger evangelicals had been privately expressing their dissatisfaction with the pastoral and theological weaknesses of the Keswick teaching for some time, while the 'Old Guard' appeared unable to respond to the main points of Packer's lucid and penetrating critique. Looking back, Packer's review can be seen to mark a turning point in evangelical attitudes on this question.

'Fundamentalism' and the Word of God *(1958)*

During his time at Tyndale Hall, Packer became heavily involved in the work of the Inter-Varsity Fellowship, the British evangelical student organisation. On average, he would speak two or three times a term at university Christian Unions around England, and gained a considerable following in the evangelical student world. In 1957, Packer was asked to give an address to the Graduates' Fellowship meeting at London with the title 'Narrow Mind – or Narrow Way?'. This title reflected a growing climate of hostility towards evangelicalism within the English churches, partly as a result of the massive Billy Graham crusades in the North London borough of Harringay in the first three months of 1954. More than two million people attended these events, which generated renewed interest in Christianity and caused a surge of numbers of people wishing to explore Christian ministry. Yet some senior church figures now openly criticised evangelicalism as anti–intellectual, holding uncritical attitudes towards reading the Bible and core Christian beliefs.

The word 'fundamentalism' now came to be widely used to refer to evangelicalism in general and the views of Billy Graham in particular. In 1956 the Bishop of Durham, Michael Ramsey, who later became Archbishop of Canterbury, wrote an article with the alarmist title 'The Menace of Fundamentalism'. He accused Billy Graham and his English followers of being lightweight and sectarian, using forms of evangelism that relied on emotional manipulation rather than reasoned argument. This, Ramsey declared, could only lead to 'the alienation of thoughtful men and women from the Christian faith'.[3] Graham's formulaic phrase 'The Bible says . . .' was seen by his critics as simplistic and potentially misleading.

John R. W. Stott, who was then emerging as a significant spokesman for the growing evangelical constituency, responded to this clamour of criticism with a pamphlet entitled *Fundamentalism and Evangelicalism*, which countered some of these attacks. He followed this through with a series of articles arguing for a judicious and thoughtful formulation of the traditional evangelical belief in the authority and trustworthiness of Scripture, helping to blunt perceptions that 'fundamentalism' was necessarily belligerent.[4] But more needed to be done. Earlier generations of English evangelicals had not given enough attention to offering a *theological* account of the authority of the Bible. A pamphlet would not be enough; it would have to be a book – one that was both theologically informed and intellectually accessible.

Those were Packer's views as he reflected on what he should do with the 7,000-word text of the lecture he had delivered at the Graduates' Fellowship meeting in London. He could publish it as a pamphlet yet every question he answered seemed to raise new questions, which simply could not be addressed in such a short space. Ronald Inchley, then Publishing Director of the Inter-Varsity Fellowship, expressed an interest in the work, and offered to consider it for publication. Inchley was clearly expecting Packer to present him with a 6,000-word text suitable for publication as a pamphlet. The package that eventually arrived on his desk in 1957, however, was a 55,000-word book.

Inchley realised that he had been presented with a challenge that was actually an opportunity. Up to that point, Inter-Varsity Fellowship had not published paperbacks. However, these were becoming increasingly popular in the secular marketplace. Penguin and Pan launched first-edition softbacks for the first time in the late 1950s. Inchley felt that the moment was right for Inter-Varsity

Fellowship to do the same, and published six titles in paperback simultaneously in 1958 as 'IVF Pocket Books'. These included John Stott's *Basic Christianity*, which went on to sell more than a million copies, and Packer's *'Fundamentalism' and the Word of God*. Both titles became landmarks in British evangelical circles, and both also achieved significant success in North America.

The importance of Packer's book lies in several of its features. For a start, it was clearly written, and engaged not only the attention of its readers but also the questions of the moment. Furthermore, Packer provided a carefully reasoned defence of an evangelical understanding of the authority of the Bible, rather than simply asserting it. While he drew on classic Protestant resources – particularly the works of the Protestant reformer John Calvin and the Princeton theologian Benjamin B. Warfield – Packer was careful to address contemporary questions about the place of the Bible, particularly those raised by A. G. Hebert in his 1957 book *Fundamentalism and the Church of God*.[5]

Packer had already chosen a title for his book: *The Faith Once Delivered*. Inchley, however, felt a more provocative title was needed, signalling the work's significance for the controversies of the day. Packer's sustained critique of Hebert's book led Inchley to suggest the title *'Fundamentalism' and the Word of God*. The deliberate use of quotation marks around the word 'fundamentalism' was intended to call into question the legitimacy of using what was seen as a disparaging and inappropriate term to refer to mainline evangelicalism. As Packer saw it, 'fundamentalism' was a theological modernist's deliberately provocative and pejorative way of referring to what he saw as the evangelical 'maintenance, in opposition to modernism, of traditional orthodox beliefs'.[6]

Packer's extended argument in this work went beyond the authority of the Bible to touch on wider issues – such as how the Bible is to be presented in order to communicate effectively with modern culture: 'Our business is to present the Christian faith clothed in modern terms, not to propagate modern thought clothed in Christian terms. Our business is to interpret and criticize modern thought by the gospel, not vice versa.'[7] Packer was also careful to note that asserting the authority of the Bible does not predetermine how the Bible is to be interpreted, nor does it 'flatten' the various distinctive literary genres found in it.

Packer's book was an important landmark in his career. Up to that point, he had been seen primarily as an advocate of Puritan theology and spirituality, with an expertise in John Owen and Richard Baxter. While both these writers are noted in *'Fundamentalism' and the Word of God*, they play only a small part in its argument. The two writers who play the most significant role in shaping Packer's thesis are John Calvin and Benjamin B. Warfield. Packer here emerges as a scholar capable of developing a critical yet constructive account of a subject important to all evangelicals, rather than the somewhat smaller group who particularly admired the Puritans.

This, I must emphasise, is about a change in the way in which Packer was *perceived*. Packer did not suddenly reinvent himself as a mainstream evangelical theologian, rooted in the Reformed tradition, having hitherto lived and moved within a Puritan theological subculture. He did indeed have a particular liking and respect for the Puritans, but saw this as enriching and informing, not displacing, his evangelical convictions. Packer offered 'a constructive re-statement of evangelical principles', which both defended mainstream evangelicals against the charge of being 'fundamentalists', while at the same time showing evangelicals that they did not need to be fundamentalists in order to affirm and enact the authority of the Bible.

But we must here return to Packer's admiration for the Puritans, which led him to intervene in a debate that began to cause anxiety to many evangelicals in the late 1950s. Many were grateful to Billy Graham for his evangelistic ministry in England in the first part of that decade; yet some awkward theological questions were raised, and not entirely resolved, by that ministry. To understand these concerns, consider this characteristic passage from Graham's *How to be Born Again*:

> God will not force His way into your life. The Holy Spirit will do everything possible to disturb you, draw you, love you – but finally it is your personal decision . . . He gave the Holy Spirit to convict you of your need. He gives the Holy Spirit to draw you to the

cross, but even after all of this, it is your decision whether to accept God's free pardon or to continue in your lost condition.[8]

It was a powerful and popular message. Nevertheless, it left unanswered the question of the nature and extent of God's involvement in human conversion, presenting it as a purely human decision whether to accept or decline God's pardon. How can a sinful human being either recognise the need to come to God, or break free from the power of sin to receive God?

This, it must be said, is still a topic for debate among Christians, and it is not something that can be fully addressed here. There have been, and remain, important divergences of opinion within Christianity over this matter. Billy Graham's evangelistic rhetoric raised particular issues for the Reformed theological tradition, which places an emphasis upon God's initiative and sovereignty in all spheres, including conversion. Packer turned to deal with these in his second book *Evangelism and the Sovereignty of God* (1961), which is now seen as a classic study on the relationship between God's sovereignty and the necessity of evangelism. Once more, we find him setting out a critical yet constructive theological proposal, aimed at resolving some tensions and difficulties that were emerging within student Christian circles in the mid-1950s. Let's look more closely at this book and its context.

Evangelism and the Sovereignty of God *(1961)*

Packer began to engage the question of evangelism seriously in 1955, when he delivered a paper on 'Puritan Evangelism'. There were, Packer suggested, several different understandings of evangelism, such as the approach developed by the American Charles G. Finney in the 1820s which took the form of an 'intensive evangelistic campaign' and the 'anxious seat' – a front pew that was left vacant so that those who felt moved by the evangelistic address could come forward for counselling. 'Finney regarded evangelistic preaching as a battle of wills between himself and his hearers, in which it was his responsibility to bring them to breaking point.'[9]

For Packer, Finney's approach to evangelism is essentially Pelagian: a battle to win people over to the Christian faith by force of argument. The grace of God plays no role in Finney's approach. Earlier, I noted how Packer suspected the Keswick holiness teaching of ultimately resting on a Pelagian view of human nature; by 1955, he had also come to share Benjamin B. Warfield's view that aggressive evangelistic campaigns such as Finney's were likewise essentially based on a Pelagian foundation. Packer was careful to point out that this did not imply that all evangelists were Pelagians; his concern was to note this as a potential danger.

The second approach to evangelism noted by Packer is that of the Puritans. This does not involve demands for an immediate decision for Christ, but rather takes the form of a sustained preaching of the gospel over an extended period of time. 'Preachers are to declare God's mind as set forth in the texts they expound, to show the way of salvation, to exhort the unconverted to learn the law, to meditate on the Word, to humble themselves, to pray that God will show them their sins, and enable them to come to Christ.'[10] Packer points out that Puritans do not think in terms of specifically evangelistic forms of preaching, but rather see evangelism as an integral element of the preacher's task: 'Evangelistic preaching is not a special kind of preaching, with its own distinctive technique. It is a part of the ordinary public ministry of God's Word.'[11]

Packer set out his concerns about some influential evangelical approaches to evangelism in his 1959 lecture 'The Puritan View of Preaching the Gospel', delivered on 15 December at Westminster Chapel. Although neither Charles Finney nor Billy Graham are mentioned in this lecture, Packer expressed concern that, while 'psychological pressures, skilfully handled, may produce the outward form of "decision", they cannot bring about regeneration and a change of heart'.[12] Approaches to evangelism which insist on an immediate response to the gospel can be counter-productive:

> Evangelism must rather be conceived as a long-term enterprise of patient teaching and instruction, in which God's servants seek simply to be faithful in delivering the gospel message and applying it to human lives, and leave it to God's Spirit to draw

men to faith through this message in His own way and at His own speed.

Yet Packer also noted an emerging and a worrying trend. Perhaps reacting against the theological unsophistication of Billy Graham, some were now arguing that the central Reformed doctrine that faith and repentance were given only to the elect was fundamentally incompatible with the public proclamation of the gospel. This became a particular issue in evangelical student circles in London in 1959, when the London Inter-Faculty Christian Union (LIFCU) set about planning a mission. Such events in the past had been very successful. In 1947, the LIFCU organised 170 student meetings across London, typically with audiences of between five and six hundred. But it soon became clear that there were now significant differences within the leadership of the LIFCU over whether it should encourage or organise any form of evangelism. Some held that no theological justification could be offered for vigorous evangelistic activity, or for making evangelistic appeals to the audience. Others believed it was unthinkable that there should not be some form of appeal.

Given his high profile in student circles, Packer was invited to speak at a pre-mission meeting arranged for 24 October 1959 at Westminster Chapel, to address and attempt to resolve the disputes involved. It was clear to Packer that this issue would not go away and needed a thorough airing. He therefore expanded his short talk into the book *Evangelism and the Sovereignty of God*. Realising that the issue of evangelism was of especial importance in student circles, he again arranged for the work to be published by the Inter-Varsity Fellowship. (It was not until 1969 that Inchley launched InterVarsity Press as the rebranded IVF publishing operation.)

The book's core argument is easily summarised. The Bible's teaching relating to the book's core theme may be stated as follows: human beings are responsible creatures, and God is sovereign. Packer has no difficulty in assembling an arsenal of biblical texts in support of these two statements. The question is how they are to be held together when they appear to be in tension with each other, if not mutually contradictory. We assume that divine sovereignty and human responsibility are incompatible; in fact, this reflects our limited grasp of these truths, and our excessive reliance on the standards of human wisdom. Packer asks us to make it 'our business to believe both these doctrines with all our might, and to keep both constantly before us for the guidance and government of our lives'.[13]

Packer frames this approach by asserting that simultaneously affirming divine sovereignty and human responsibility represents an 'antinomy' – that is to say, 'an appearance of contradiction between conclusions which seem equally logical, reasonable or necessary'.[14] As he notes, this causes us rational discomfort since 'To our finite minds this is inexplicable.'[15] So why does this perception of inconsistency arise? Packer notes four factors that create difficulties for us at this point: an unhelpful intrusion of rationalistic speculations; an understandable but misplaced passion for systematic consistency; a reluctance to acknowledge the existence of mystery and allow that God is wiser than we are; and the improper imposition of human logic on the interpretation of the Bible.

Packer rightly notes that we like to tie up everything into 'neat intellectual parcels', with all appearance of mystery dispelled and no loose ends dangling at any point. For this reason, we are often tempted to eliminate antinomies from our minds by questionable and misguided means – such as suppressing or abandoning one truth in the supposed interests of the other, and for the sake of a neater and tidier theology. 'What should one do, then, with an antinomy? Accept it for what it is, and learn to live with it.'[16]

Packer's resolution of this tension – learning to live with these two fundamental principles, affirming both and holding them together in our reflections and actions – means we should refuse to regard the apparent inconsistency as real, and must attribute an appearance of contradiction to the deficiency of our own understanding. We should not think of the two principles as rival alternatives, but as being *complementary* to each other in a way that we cannot fully understand. Christians are called to think and live within the creative tension of these two core affirmations, holding them together in a balanced unity and exploring how they are to be applied. Packer is thus critical of those who give an excessive – and occasionally exclusive – emphasis to human responsibility, and others who give too much weight to divine sovereignty.

As an example of the second error, Packer reminds his readers of the response of some of the audience to William Carey's suggestion in 1786 that missionaries should be sent out to unevangelised areas of the world. 'Sit down, young man, when God is pleased to convert the heathen, he will do it without your help or mine!' As Packer noted, a misplaced zeal to glorify God and to acknowledge his sovereign grace can all too easily lead us to lose sight of the Church's responsibility to evangelise. YES~ matt 28

For Packer, it is our duty to proclaim salvation, while never losing sight of the fact that it is God who saves: 'Our evangelistic work is the instrument that he uses for this purpose, but the power that saves is not in the instrument: it is in the hand of the One who uses the instrument.'[17] His insistence that we hold together human responsibility and divine sovereignty recognises that these two principles often seem to pull in opposite directions. For Packer, if we cannot entirely resolve that tension, we can at least agree to live with and work within its framework.

Packer also made a point that many noted with interest. The New Testament, he suggested, did not lay down precise stipulations on how best to go about evangelistic preaching, or developing an evangelistic ministry.

> The best method of evangelism is the one which serves the gospel most completely . . . which bears the clearest witness to the divine origin of the message . . . which makes possible the most full and thorough explanation of the good news of Christ and his cross . . . YES which most effectively engages the minds of those to whom witness is borne . . . What that best method is in each case, you and I have to find out for ourselves.[18]

Rather than lay down a normative template, Packer set out some guidelines that would enable entrepreneurial ministers to develop and share their own methods, adapted to their own gifts and situations.

Moving On

Packer was clearly a valued and respected member of the teaching staff of Tyndale Hall. When I was researching my biography of Packer back in the 1990s, I got in touch with many of his students from Tyndale, who shared their memories of Packer's approach to teaching theology and how it had affected their ministry and preaching. One of the things they particularly treasured about Packer was his willingness to talk about theology over the college breakfast table. The students would ask him about the great theological questions of the day – the relationship between divine sovereignty and human freedom, to give one obvious example. Packer did not give them pre-packaged answers; instead, he showed his theological working. In effect, Packer taught them how to *theologise* – how to *do* theology, rather than simply presenting them with the outcomes of that process. It was a rare gift, and one that Packer would consolidate over his long career as a teacher.

But although Packer was happy at Tyndale Hall, his growing reputation as an informed, constructive and critical exponent of evangelicalism was beginning to open up new horizons for him. The publication of his two books secured him a significant national and international profile. He was clearly marked for a position of intellectual leadership. But where? And what form might this take?

We shall pick up our narrative shortly. Once more, however, we need to pause as we survey Packer's career to consider his thoughts about the place of the Bible in Christian life and thought. Being such a major theme of Packer's ministry, it demands further reflection and exploration.

6

The Bible: Authority,
Interpretation and Translation

During his time as tutor in doctrine at Tyndale Hall, Bristol, Packer gained a reputation as a careful and thoughtful theologian who tried to weave together the Bible and Christian theology, refusing to see them as separate and non-interacting compartments of the Christian mind. He has maintained this position throughout his career. The large archive of recordings of Packer's presentations at Regent College, Vancouver, includes a rich array of items on systematic theology, spirituality and biblical exposition. For example, in the summer of 2016 he offered two courses of lectures at the Regent College summer school: one on the Anglican heritage; the other on Paul's Letter to the Colossians. There is always a risk that systematic theology becomes independent of the Bible. Packer's principled attentiveness towards the biblical text is a clear theological virtue for evangelical writers and preachers.

I benefited from his wisdom in the early 1990s, when I served as general editor of the *NIV Thematic Study Bible*. This work set out to help its readers identify the great themes that criss-cross the books of the Bible, as an aid to preaching and personal devotion. It was a substantial work and needed the advice of someone who knew the biblical texts well and recognised the importance in bringing out the Bible's theological and spiritual unity. Packer agreed to act as a consultant editor to help forge and consolidate the vision for the project. It was obvious that this was something close to his heart, and the whole project was enriched by his advice and encouragement.[1]

Packer also played a significant role in developing the *English Standard Version*, a new translation of the Bible published in 2001.[2] Like any good Protestant writer, Packer insisted that the Bible must be understood by its readers. Every Christian ought to have access to the text of the Bible, even if they were unfamiliar with the chief biblical languages of Greek and Hebrew. Packer himself preferred more literal translations of the biblical text, such as the *English Standard Version*, aware that paraphrases tended to conceal genuine issues of interpretation.

How, then, does Packer integrate the Bible into his vision of Christian life and thought? One of the first publishing projects with which Packer became involved was writing a series of articles for the *New Bible Dictionary*. This major work traced its origins back to a proposal of 1953, which noted the need for a new Bible 'dictionary and/or encyclopaedia'. Initially, the publishing division of the Inter-Varsity Fellowship in London considered updating an existing American edition, before deciding that a completely new work was required. James D. Douglas (Editor-at-Large for *Christianity Today*) was duly appointed as editor, with F. F. Bruce (Rylands Professor of Biblical Criticism and Exegesis at the University of Manchester), R. V. G. Tasker (Professor of New Testament Exegesis at King's College London), D. J. Wiseman (Professor of Assyriology at the University of London), and Packer as consultant editors.

Packer was the least experienced of the team of editors, but quickly proved his worth. It was a major undertaking, both in terms of planning the structure of the project and commissioning the articles themselves. The work was not published until 1962, when it established itself as a major resource. Packer himself contributed eighteen articles on topics such as 'Authority', 'Conversion', 'Earnest', 'Election', 'Incarnation', 'Inspiration', 'Predestination' and 'Revelation'.

More than fifty years later, Packer was again involved in the production of detailed studies of aspects of the Bible. As theological editor of the 2,750-page *English Standard Version Study Bible* (2008), he was responsible for a series of detailed annotations to the biblical text, helping readers understand the meaning of specific passages. Yet this attention to detail never distracted Packer from something more important – seeing the 'bigger picture', of which these individual details were a part. In 2018, Packer set out some principles which he himself found helpful in reading the Bible and grasping its full significance.

Most importantly, get the big picture. Don't worry too much at
first about specific sentences you don't quite understand. The
details fit when you've got the big picture. That is my first and
fundamental exhortation with regard to Bible reading and
study.[3]

Packer here sets out a way of reading Scripture which respects the
unique place of the Bible, while at the same time helping us understand the role of theology in distilling and safeguarding its central
themes.

Packer's basic point is simple: enjoy looking at the trees – but
make sure you can see the forest as well. Packer put this well in his
2008 introduction to 'Reading the Bible Theologically' in the *English
Standard Version Study Bible*: 'Scripture is no ragbag of religious bits
and pieces, unrelated to each other; rather, it is a tapestry in which
all the complexities of the weave display a single pattern of judgment
and mercy, promise and fulfilment.'[4]

This has been a constant theme of Packer's writings since 1954.
Theology, he pointed out in one of his earliest articles, is a unitary
discipline, which is grounded in and expresses the fundamental unity
of Scripture as a whole.[5] The details of individual biblical passages
and themes matter – but so does the bigger picture, which positions
each of these details in proper context and allows its overall significance to be better appreciated.[6]

So how is this 'big picture' developed and applied? Although
Packer uses several frameworks to explore this question, one of his
earliest focuses on the journey from biblical *exegesis* to theological
synthesis and finally to practical *application*.[7] The first stage is *exegesis*.
Packer understands this as 'bringing out of the text' – not reading
into the text! – all that it contains of 'the whole expressed mind' of
the biblical writer. This leads into *synthesis* – a 'process of gathering
up, and surveying in historically integrated form, the fruits of exegesis'. And finally, this in turn leads to *application*, in which the preacher
asks what God might say and do to us, given what God said and did
in the past.

So important is this theme of the theological synthesis of Scripture
to Packer that he explores and expounds it at multiple points in his

works. Consider, for example, this particularly lucid exploration from a 1991 article considering the relation of theology and spirituality:

> The first task is exegetical. Treating the biblical material as God's own didactic witness to himself, given in the form of the didactic witness to him of the Bible writers, we are to draw from the canonical text everything we can find relating to the Creator, and receive it as pure truth from God's own mouth . . . The second task . . . is synthetic. All the data about God that exegesis has established must be brought together in a single coherent scheme, just as a historian schematizes all his facts into a single flowing narrative.[8]

Packer's point is that biblical threads need to be woven together to disclose and display a theological pattern; that is to say, according to Packer, a way of reading the Bible 'with a focus on God'. Back in 1985, Packer found a neat way of expressing this approach: he was 'first and foremost a theological exegete'.[9]

Precisely what does Packer mean by this? And how does he understand the relation of theology and the Bible? Many have expressed concern that the academic discipline of systematic theology often seems to proceed without any sense of connection with, or dependence upon, biblical texts. Packer, however, sees a seamless and organic connection between the practice of theologising – an active verbal form that he frequently prefers over the static noun 'theology' – and the reading of Scripture.

> I can schematize my use of the Bible in theologizing as follows. I make use of the Bible (1) in personal devotion, (2) in preaching and pastoral ministry, (3) in academic theological work. Use (3) underlies use (2) and is fed by use (1). I approach the Bible in all three connections as the communication of doctrine from God; as the instrument of Jesus Christ's personal authority over Christians (which is part of what I mean in calling it canonical); as the criterion of truth and error regarding God and godliness; as wisdom for the ordering of life and food for spiritual growth.[10]

Packer's approach (which he finds especially in the writings of John Calvin and John Owen) affirms the central importance of the Christian Bible, while insisting on the need to take intellectual trouble to ensure that both preaching and theology present an integrated, not fragmented, account of the larger vision of reality that lies within the biblical texts – 'a total, integrated view built out of biblical material'.[11] And such an 'integrated view' serves both to maintain Christian identity and act as a criticism of prevailing – yet ultimately *shifting* – secular norms which can only too easily become incorporated into Christian thinking. It is, Packer warns, facile to convert 'the study of sacred theology into a venture in secular ideology'. Like C. S. Lewis, Packer expresses concern about an 'intellectual idolatry which absolutizes the axioms of contemporary culture'.[12]

Yet 'theological exegesis' is a process that ultimately rests on a theological understanding of the Bible. As we saw when considering *'Fundamentalism' and the Word of God* in the previous chapter, Packer was also concerned to establish a solid theological foundation for understanding the distinct identity and purpose of the Bible. In what way was the Bible to be distinguished from other religious books? What was different about it? Packer has consistently contended that the Bible is to be seen as inspired by God, using individual human authors to bear witness to the nature and purpose of God.

> All Scripture is witness to God, given by divinely illuminated human writers, and all Scripture is God witnessing to himself in and through their words. The way into the mind of God is through the expressed mind of these human writers, so the reader of the Bible looks for that characteristic first. But the text must be read, or reread, as God's own self-revelatory instruction, given in the form of this human testimony.[13]

Linked with this is Packer's insistence on the need for the guidance of the Holy Spirit in the interpretation of the Bible. Noting that the term 'illumination' is often used to refer to this aspect of the work of the Spirit, Packer comments that such illumination 'is not a giving of new revelation, but a work within us that enables us to grasp and to love the revelation that is there before us in the biblical text as heard and read, and as explained by teachers and writers'.[14] But Packer recognises that discussions of biblical interpretation and application are often difficult, and that disputes about how to interpret biblical passages are neither resolved nor marginalised by an appeal to the notion of biblical infallibility.

> Questions of inerrancy and interpretation *must* be kept separate. Acknowledging that whatever biblical writers communicate on any subject is God-given truth does not commit you in advance to any one method or school of interpretation, nor to any one way of relating Scripture to science, nor to any one set of proposed harmonizations of inconsistent-looking texts.[15]

Evangelicals, Packer comments, sometimes let themselves speak 'as if everything immediately becomes plain and obvious for believers in biblical inerrancy, to such an extent that uncertainties about interpretation never arise for them'.[16]

One of the many criticisms often directed against evangelical interpretations of the Bible is that they tend to be highly individualist readings – what Packer himself described as a 'Lone Ranger' approach, adopted by people who have 'proudly or impatiently' turned their backs on the Church and their heritage.[17] While it is clearly important to ground biblical truth in the lives of individuals, there is a danger that individual perspectives and judgements become theologically determinative. This is the way I see things – so this is how things really are.

What, then, can be done about this? Packer stresses the importance of 'keeping regular company with yesterday's great teachers', who can help us discern wisdom that might otherwise be denied to us, and challenge us about our own skewed or biased readings of the Bible. He offers a conceptual framework which allows us to see writers like Luther, Calvin and Jonathan Edwards as helpful in informing and nourishing our faith, *without displacing or undermining the Bible itself*. To use Packer's own words, writers like Edwards can play a *ministerial*, not a *magisterial*, role in our theologising. The Puritans' reading of the Bible, and the way in which they applied it, can help us today, yet without disconnecting or distancing us from

Scripture itself. The Christian past is like a quarry; we are invited to explore, appropriate and apply its riches, critically but also positively. We can even learn from past mistakes about the interpretation of the Bible – mistakes that are sometimes made for the best of reasons.

Packer's overall vision thus holds together the core importance of the Bible itself and the long Christian process of engaging, under-standing and applying the Bible. The way in which others have 'synthesised' the core themes of the Bible can remain valuable to us today, so long as we exercise prudence and caution in assessing these. Figures of wisdom from the past can help us with biblical exegesis, with weaving together biblical threads into a theological tapestry, and with applying this theological synthesis to the basis of living. We shall explore these themes further later in this volume.

We now rejoin our narrative of Packer's life, as he reflected on what opportunities for service and ministry might lie beyond his work at Tyndale Hall, Bristol.

7

The Return to Oxford: Latimer House

Packer had no intention of staying at Tyndale Hall for the remainder of his career. It was a demanding role which he had enjoyed. Perhaps more importantly, it had allowed him to hone his skills as a theological educator, and reflect on how establishing a solid theological foundation for ministry could sustain and direct churches in times of change and uncertainty. But he needed a larger platform to develop his distinctive ministry.

A number of options were open to Packer. He might follow the paths of many former members of staff at Tyndale Hall, who had returned to ministry in parishes. Or he might seek a more senior position at another evangelical theological college of the Church of England.

A further option was suggested by his predecessor at Tyndale Hall, Geoffrey Bromiley, who had returned to parish ministry, becoming Rector of St Thomas' Church, Corstorphine, Edinburgh. However, in 1958, Bromiley had announced that he was leaving parish ministry to take up a new appointment as Professor of Church History and Historical Theology at Fuller Theological Seminary in California. As we saw earlier, Bromiley was something of a role model for Packer's vision of a theological educator. So might he also find a position at an American seminary? Packer's two books had attracted attention in Reformed seminaries in North America, making this a genuine possibility at the time.

Packer, however, felt that there was work that he still needed to do in his native England. As the 1960s got under way, many felt that Britain was going through a period of significant cultural change, with important implications for the Christian churches. Could they rise to the new challenges that were emerging? Perhaps more than any evangelical thinker other than John Stott, Packer had given considerable thought to how evangelicalism might respond to these new opportunities. In his bestselling book *Basic Christianity*, John Stott set out the case for Christianity in measured, rational terms, aiming to reassure his readers, many of whom were university students, that Christian belief was 'intellectually respectable'.[1] However, he needed a platform from which to explore further fundamental questions of ministry, preaching and outreach. Stott had made All Souls, Langham Place, London, his podium for engaging both Church and nation.[2] Was there such a platform for Packer? Initially, there was not. But that, as things worked out, was about to change.

In December 1958, John Wenham – a close colleague of Packer, and then Vice Principal of Tyndale Hall, Bristol – wrote a memorandum setting out a vision for an 'Evangelical Research Centre' in Oxford. I got to know Wenham well at Oxford in the 1980s, and he often reflected with me on the importance of evangelical research institutions, telling me how he and Packer played a key role in bringing one into being in Oxford. Wenham noted that Cambridge already had such an institution in Tyndale House, which had been founded as an interdenominational evangelical centre for the study of the New Testament. Wenham suggested that there was a need for a comparable evangelical institution in Oxford, although differing from Tyndale House in two important respects. First, it would be a specifically Anglican centre; and second, it would focus on issues such as doctrine, worship and church polity. Packer regarded Wenham's idea of an Anglican evangelical research centre as inspired, and argued that its creation was 'a strategic requirement of the very highest priority'.[3]

Plans were made to raise funds for what came to be known as the Oxford Evangelical Research Trust. Wenham and Packer were part of the organising committee, which was chaired by John Stott. By January 1960, funds were in place to allow the purchase of 131 Banbury Road, a large house just north of Oxford city centre, and appoint two resident members of staff: a Warden and a Librarian. The initiative would have three core aims: to provide opportunities for study and writing for its two staff members; to organise a select fellowship of Anglican scholars to work together on important projects; and to strengthen the evangelical witness in Oxford.

It was decided that the first Warden would be Richard J. Coates, a colleague of Packer's at Tyndale Hall. With the benefit of hindsight, this was a surprising choice, which did not entirely match up with the core objectives of the proposed research centre. Coates combined his part-time teaching of liturgy at Tyndale with the incumbency of Christ Church, a parish in the nearby seaside resort of Weston-super-Mare. He was not well known, and had no track record of research or publishing. The centre's first Librarian would be Philip E. Hughes. It was also agreed that, given his obvious talents, Packer would be invited to work for the centre for two days a week. Hopes were high for the centre, which would be known as 'Latimer House' after the Protestant scholar-bishop Hugh Latimer. Latimer – along with Thomas Cranmer and Nicolas Ridley – was an 'Oxford Martyr' who was burned at the stake in the middle of Oxford in 1555.

Unfortunately, things quickly began to go wrong for Latimer House. Coates and Hughes fell out with each other and decided they could not both live in the same building. In June 1960, Hughes resigned as Librarian. The Council made a good decision and invited Packer to take Hughes' place. For contractual reasons, Packer would be unable to take up the position until April 1961. On his arrival in Oxford, Coates told Packer that he was on the brink of resigning as Warden, and intended to leave as soon as he could find suitable alternative employment. After some discussion, the Council decided to appoint Packer as Warden, and, at Packer's suggestion, Roger Beckwith as Librarian. By the middle of 1962, the new team was in place, and Latimer House was finally ready to do business.

Although Latimer House provided Packer with a platform for theological engagement with the life of the churches, it did not itself have any institutional connection with the local churches. Packer remedied this deficiency by becoming involved in the ministry of St Andrews, Linton Road, a large evangelical parish church in north Oxford close to Latimer House. For Packer, this was an important expression of his deep commitment to the ministerial aspects of theology.

Honest to God: Latimer House and the Shaping of Evangelical Opinion

Packer's vision for Latimer House comes close to what would now be described as a 'think tank', concerned with research and knowledge dissemination at the interface between theology and the life of the Church. In commending the creation of an evangelical research centre in Oxford, Packer stressed that it should not seek to promote 'ivory tower scholarship' but should rather engage the 'actual present-day needs of Anglican evangelicalism'. Although many evangelicals feared the cultural and theological liberalising agendas of certain bishops of the Church of England, there was no expectation of any immediate crises arising into which evangelicalism would need to make a considered and powerful intervention.

Without warning, however, a crisis came in March 1963. John Robinson, Bishop of Woolwich, contributed an article to a leading British Sunday newspaper with the provocative title – almost certainly chosen by one of the newspaper's editors – 'Our Image of God must go'. Robinson's demands for radical theological revisionism were set out in his book *Honest to God*, published four days later. Probably on account of the sensationalist newspaper publicity, it became a bestseller in England and earned the nickname 'Honest John' for its author.[4] The initial print run ordered by the publishers was a mere 8,000 copies, of which 2,000 were intended for export to the United States. The print run sold out on the first day of publication. The demand for the book took everyone by surprise. It is estimated that the book sold 350,000 copies during its first seven months.

Honest to God caused outrage and hand-wringing in the Church of England at the time of its publication, not least because the media depicted Robinson as writing off traditional Christian beliefs as outdated, irrelevant and meaningless relics of a bygone era. Robinson, who lacked significant experience in dealing with the press, failed to establish – or even to *attempt* to establish – a credible alternative media narrative. The Archbishop of Canterbury stepped in to denounce the book as a caricature of Christian views of God. Evangelicals were particularly outraged that a bishop should write a book ridiculing and rejecting Christian orthodoxy and still be allowed to remain in office. Yet these responses were framed at the institutional level and failed to engage with Robinson's basic presuppositions and methods. It was clear that a *theological* critique of *Honest to God* was called for.

Packer immediately grasped that both he as a theologian, and Latimer House as a theological research centre focusing on issues affecting the Church of England, were strategically placed to intervene in this debate. What was needed was a short and accessible response to *Honest to God* which concentrated on Robinson's ideas, rather than debating whether he had misused his position as a bishop. Packer knew he could do this. His compact rebuttal of *Honest to God*, a mere twenty pages in length, was published later that same year.[5] While Packer welcomed Robinson's pastoral and apologetic concerns in addressing some of the cultural anxieties of his age, he considered that Robinson's intervention had failed to answer such concerns properly. What Robinson proposed was not merely an inadequate response to some genuine apologetic questions, but also a dilution, if not a distortion, of Christianity.

Packer's theological critique is entirely justified. Robinson shows little awareness of the patristic discussions of the identity and significance of Jesus Christ, which led to the formulation of the 'Chalcedonian Definition' of Christ as truly divine and truly human. Robinson insists that the Chalcedonian approach leads to the notion of Christ as 'a divine visitant from "out there", who chooses to live in every respect like the natives'.[6] But this was at best a very muddled misunderstanding of Chalcedonian orthodoxy, which both tainted Robinson's faulty assessment of contemporary difficulties with classic Christology and led him to formulate some thoroughly inadequate alternatives.

Packer's focus was fundamentally theological, identifying Robinson's hasty scholarly misjudgements and their deeply problematic outcomes. Robinson had created a mish-mash of three very different German theological voices – Rudolf Bultmann, Dietrich Bonhoeffer and Paul Tillich. Bultmann argued for the 'demythologisation' of the New Testament text, so that its core themes could be understood in existential terms; Bonhoeffer brought home the rise of secular understandings of human existence, encapsulated in the phrase 'religionless Christianity'; and, clearly most importantly for Robinson, Tillich invited us to revise our idea of God in terms of a 'Ground of Being' or 'Being-itself'. Yet Robinson never managed to integrate these dissonant voices, nor to coordinate them in an apologetically focused way, capable of retaining or re-expressing the central insights of Christian orthodoxy. Packer's caustic assessment of *Honest to God* has stood the test of time well: 'it is just a plateful of mashed-up Tillich fried in Bultmann and garnished with Bonhoeffer'.[7] Every page of the work bore the unmistakable 'marks of unfinished thinking'.

It is not difficult to endorse Packer's concerns. Robinson called for a wholesale revision of the Christian faith, declaring that 'the most fundamental categories of our theology – of God, of the supernatural, and of religion itself – must go into the melting'.[8] Yet although Robinson presented himself as a radical, demanding that we return to the New Testament to recover a more authentic vision of Christianity, his reading of the New Testament is driven by a modernist worldview and a somewhat superficial understanding of Tillich's existential thesis: 'The transcendent is nothing external or "out there" but is encountered in, with and under the Thou of all finite relationships as their ultimate depth and ground and meaning.'[9] Packer concluded that we are forced to choose between two incompatible visions of God – 'a God who is personal and a Father, and a God who is neither, but simply an aspect of ourselves'.[10]

Packer was concerned not simply with the inadequate foundations of Robinson's theology however; he relentlessly pointed out its unacceptable consequences. Robinson's theology had no place for the concepts of God as Creator or Redeemer. Robinson's Jesus could not in any meaningful sense be termed 'Saviour' or 'Lord'. He had created a complete disjunction between theology and worship. Robinson's God 'has done nothing to be praised for'. It was no surprise that Robinson redefined worship in terms of a preparation for service of other people, rather than primarily as a response to God's being and deeds, which in turn motivates and inspires us to serve others.

Dr. Robinson's programme seems to be that Christians should (i) agree with modern man that historic Christianity is irrelevant to him, but (ii) tell him that he is not, and cannot be, an atheist, since his 'ultimate concern' (whatever that may be) is 'God'. A non-Tillichite may be forgiven for feeling that this is more of a policy for calling worldlings Christians than for making them such.[11]

Packer's response to Robinson was not a bestseller and was never intended to be. Its object was to challenge Robinson's faulty apologetics at a theological level, and thus serve the Church – especially the growing evangelical constituency within the Church of England. By January 1964, the work had sold 20,000 copies. Latimer House had proved itself capable of rising to a new and, it may be added, unexpected challenge. Its contribution to the *Honest to God* controversy resonated with the concerns raised by other leading Christians, and opened up possibilities for alliances and conversations based on classic orthodox Christianity. The Anglo-Catholic writer E. L. Mascall, for example, confirmed Packer's estimation of the book, noting that if 'Robinson is right in saying that "God is teaching us that we must live as men who can get on very well without Him", then the Church has no need to say anything whatever to secularized man, for that is precisely what secularized man already believes'.[12]

But Packer realised that, despite the obvious success of Latimer House's intervention in this specific debate, it had exposed some weaknesses in its ability to undertake long-term planning for the future. In a report to the Latimer House Council, Packer noted that the *Honest to God* controversy had shown that Latimer House was 'vulnerable to unforeseen developments'. Even writing such a short book was demanding, requiring time and attention that inevitably meant that other tasks and responsibilities had to be neglected. It was difficult to undertake long-term planning for Latimer House's ministry, given this need to react to urgent needs for intervention. Scholarship was, Packer suggested, a slow process, making the rapid production of considered and substantial responses to controversial works or issues somewhat difficult. It was therefore necessary to identify priorities – such as the theological resourcing of the growing evangelical movement within the Church of England.

Latimer House and the Theological Consolidation of Anglican Evangelicalism

One of Packer's longer term aims for Latimer House was to provide theological support and resources for more conservative forms of evangelicalism as these became increasingly significant in the life of the Church of England during the 1960s. Post-war English evangelicalism was a complex and shifting amalgam, with several elements. One important element was located outside the Church of England – the free and independent churches associated with the Fellowship of Independent Evangelical Churches. By far the most important thinker within this tradition was Dr Martyn Lloyd-Jones, minister of Westminster Chapel, London.

Within the Church of England, two main forms of evangelicalism jostled alongside each other during the 1950s: a dwindling band of liberal evangelicals associated with the Anglican Evangelical Group Movement, and an expanding group of conservative evangelicals, represented by John R. W. Stott and Packer himself.[13] During the 1960s, liberal evangelicalism struggled to articulate its vision and offer strong leadership. Partly as a result of numerical expansion arising from the Billy Graham crusades, and partly on account of its more strategic approach to theological and institutional leadership, conservative evangelicalism became increasingly prominent in the life of the Church of England. Packer saw Latimer House as a resource which would ensure that numerical growth would not result in theological shallowness.

An issue of particular importance was the theological education of evangelical clergy within the Church of England. A growing number of people who were converted through Graham's evangelistic ministry felt they were being called to serve in full-time ministry in the Church of England. For Packer, it was vital that these clergy were not merely evangelistically enthusiastic; they needed to be theologically informed if they were to meet the new challenges that awaited them.

Packer's own experience of theological education as a student at Wycliffe Hall, Oxford, and as a theological educationalist at Oak Hill College and Tyndale Hall, Bristol, had helped him identify challenges which he believed needed to be met. It was not enough to address the practical side of training for ministry – for example, through immersion in the culture of the Church of England or gaining experience of preaching and pastoral care. While these were clearly important, future clergy should be required to supplement them by developing a *theological* vision for their ministry, grounding their work in a deep understanding and appreciation of the gospel.

Much attention at this time focused on the contemporary relevance of the Thirty-Nine Articles of the Church of England (1563). These were drawn up during the reign of Elizabeth I, whose 'Settlement of Religion' is widely seen as establishing the distinct identity of the Church of England. The Articles were always regarded as subordinate to the creeds, in effect identifying what was distinctive about the Church of England, not what was definitive for Christianity as a whole.

Although some Anglicans suggest that the Thirty-Nine Articles develop a 'middle way (*via media*)' between Catholicism and Protestantism, a more accurate historical judgement is that they actually construct an Anglican middle way positioned somewhere between the beliefs and practices of two forms of Protestantism that were influential in the 1560s, namely, the Lutheran and the Reformed churches.[14] While the Articles themselves are somewhat brief, there was a clear expectation that any ambiguities or omissions would be sorted out through the theologically normative *Book of Homilies*, a collection of 'approved' sermons issued by Thomas Cranmer during the reign of Edward VI in 1547. Article Thirty-Five explicitly references and endorses these sermons, as well as a later collection assembled by Bishop John Jewel and others in 1571.

At this stage in his career, Packer saw the Thirty-Nine Articles as serving two important functions: first, as a guide to the fundamental themes of classic Anglicanism; and second, as a crucial bulwark against the rising tide of liberalism within the English national Church during the 1960s. For Packer, the Thirty-Nine Articles are to be seen as:

Time-honoured judgements, on specific issues relating to the faith of Christ, as set forth in the Scriptures. They come to us as corporate decisions first made by the Church centuries ago, and now confirmed and commended to us by the corroborative testimony of all later generations that have accepted them, down to our time.[15]

Packer's overall argument consisted of two basic assertions. First, that the Thirty-Nine Articles embody the historic theological heritage of the Church of England, and thus must be taken very seriously in any discussion of contemporary Anglican identity and theology; and second, that evangelical Anglicans, in taking these Articles to heart, were demonstrating their true Anglican credentials – unlike those who wanted to replace this historic formulation of faith with something more appropriate to the 'spirit of the age' of the 1960s.

Packer thus set out to highlight the value of the Thirty-Nine Articles in providing a theological foundation and direction for a resurgent evangelicalism within the Church of England. At that time, the most widely read evangelical Anglican publication was the *Church of England Newspaper*. Packer therefore arranged to set out his views on the ongoing importance of the Thirty-Nine Articles in a series of six substantial pieces published in this newspaper during October and November 1960. Encouraged by their positive reception, Packer brought them together as a booklet the following year.[16] The Articles, Packer declared, 'sought to confess, preserve and mark off the deepened understanding of the biblical faith which the Reformation had brought about', setting out a positive vision of 'the biblical gospel and biblical Christianity'. As evangelicalism began its long and slow consolidation within the Church of England during this period, Packer insisted that it should remain faithful to the foundational vision of that Church, as it emerged from the Reformation.

Packer was not on his own here. Many evangelicals within the Church of England around this time perceived the Thirty-Nine Articles as rooting the national Church in Scripture, and thus demonstrating that the 'church's authority never floats free of Scripture, and can never be posited independently of Scripture, as though it could dispense with its text and establish its own commentary irrespective of what the text contained'.[17] Yet during the 1960s, many clergy in the Church of England regarded statements of faith originating from the Tudor period as outdated liabilities, incapable of relating to the thought-world of the modern age, centred on the present experience of individuals. Evangelicals realised that their first line of defence against the threat of liberal theological encroachment was to reaffirm the importance of the Articles in defining the essence of Anglicanism.[18]

It was, however, a tactic, rather than a strategy. What was really needed was not a critique of the historical credentials of Anglican liberalism, but a compelling demonstration of the intellectual, moral and imaginative appeal of orthodox Christianity to those caught up in the rapid cultural transitions of the 1960s. Billy Graham might have spoken persuasively and effectively in 1954; British culture, though, had moved on, and new strategies were required to deal with the changed cultural context. During the 1950s and early 1960s, several leading evangelical churches generated local experiments in developing such apologetic and evangelistic strategies adapted to the cultural shifts of the age – for instance, those put in place by John Stott at All Souls, Langham Place, London.[19]

Latimer House played a significant role in this process of reflection, supplementing such local initiatives with a flurry of publications relating to the challenges and opportunities of the day. At the Council meeting of 25 June 1966, Packer announced plans for four further monographs. He intended to write two himself: *British Theology in the Twentieth Century* and *Theology of the Thirty-Nine Articles*; two would be written by Roger Beckwith, the House's Librarian: *Principles of Prayer Book Revision* and *Christian Initiation*. Packer found himself increasingly in demand as a member of various official church bodies, including the Archbishop's Doctrine Commission (chaired at this stage by Bishop Ian Ramsey), the Faith and Order Advisory Group, and the dialogue groups between Anglicanism and other churches (most notably, the Presbyterian Church and the Methodist Church).

The relentless activity of Latimer House made significant demands on its two staff, particularly Packer, who was constantly invited to speak at conferences on theological issues, to address Diocesan Evangelical Unions on matters of theology and church politics, and to preach at supportive churches. Latimer House depended on the generosity of its supporters, and part of Packer's task was to show that they were getting results for their donations.

Packer's strenuous workload at this time also caused some small degree of disagreement between him and the Council of Latimer House over what their priorities should be. Should he accept overseas speaking engagements, such as a major invitation to Fuller Theological Seminary, Pasadena, in 1965? Packer felt that such engagements would enhance the profile of Latimer House internationally, and broaden his own experience; the Council was unsure whether this kind of international work was entirely in line with Latimer House's specific national and denominational objective of influencing the course of debates within the Church of England. In the end, Packer was allowed to go to Pasadena. Indeed, this invitation made it clear that Packer was becoming an international voice in evangelical discussions, whereas Latimer House had a more local and focused agenda, based on the English context.

There was, however, plenty for Packer to do in England. The mounting strength and sophistication of evangelicalism within the Church of England was particularly evident in the debate over a proposed scheme for union between the Church of England and the Methodist Church. Packer and Latimer House played a major role in pointing out that this 1960s' debate was conducted almost entirely without reference to theological issues. At the time, the ecumenical movement had somewhat uncritically adopted the World Council of Churches' slogan 'doctrine divides; ministry unites'. Evangelicals pointed out that this deliberate evasion of doctrinal matters was thoroughly unsatisfactory, and argued that there was a need to face up to these doctrinal differences in a frank and honest manner. For Packer and others, Methodism had become deeply influenced by a theological liberalism which they had no desire to see gain the ascendency within a reconfigured Church of England. For Packer, the proposed merger scheme would simply create a liberal catholic denomination, in which the evangelical cause would be marginalised or suppressed.

Packer coordinated opposition to this scheme by assembling two collections of essays, each of which was formative in consolidating evangelical opposition to the proposed merger: *The Church of England and the Methodist Church* (1963) and *All in Each Place: Towards Reunion in England* (1965). In May 1968, Packer was joined by Colin O. Buchanan and Gervase E. Duffield in editing *Fellowship in the Gospel*, a substantial and critical evangelical analysis of two major Church of England reports, *Anglican-Methodist Unity* and *Intercommunion Today*.

In the end, these proposals for union foundered. They were exposed as institutionally premature and theologically shallow, failing to engage the deeper questions that had to be resolved. As a recent study of these debates makes clear, Packer emerged as the '*de facto* theologian-in-chief' of conservative evangelicalism,[20] who raised legitimate theological concerns that the liberal establishment hoped to sideline. The proposals were rejected by the Church Assembly (a predecessor of the Church of England's General Synod) in July 1969. Given the major divisions that have arisen since the 1990s over – to mention only one example – the ministry of women within the churches, few would now agree with the World Council of Churches' simplistic slogan 'doctrine divides; ministry unites'. This may have been plausible in the social context of the 1960s, but that cultural world has long since vanished.

Yet a new controversy soon flared up within Anglican evangelicalism, in which Packer and Latimer House would play a leading, even defining, role in the reevaluation of Anglican evangelicalism during the late 1960s, particularly through the National Evangelical Anglican Congress which took place at the University of Keele in 1967. In what follows, we shall explore how that convention came to be convened, the central role which Packer played, and its implications for the future of evangelicalism.

The Crisis of 1966: The Redefining of English Evangelicalism

Earlier, we noted the strategic alliance that developed in the 1950s between Packer and Dr Martyn Lloyd-Jones of Westminster Chapel, London. This resulted in the development of the Puritan Studies

Conference, which became of strategic importance for many evangelicals within the Church of England and the Fellowship of Independent Evangelical Churches. The Conferences enabled networking and strategic reflection on a number of issues during the post-war years, as well as quarrying the riches of Puritan theological and pastoral wisdom.

But there were tensions between these two groups over a number of issues, especially questions relating to ecclesiology. Traditionally, evangelicals managed to collaborate with each other across denominational lines through what was, in effect, a form of theological diplomacy. Issues of church policy or fundamental beliefs about the nature of the true Church were discussed through Puritan intermediaries. Yet in the early 1960s, it became clear that one specific question could not be dealt with in this way: should evangelicals concerned with doctrinal orthodoxy withdraw from denominations which publicly fail to maintain such orthodoxy, or should they try to reform them from within? This had been a major issue within American evangelicalism during the fundamentalist controversies of the 1920s. Although this debate had little impact in the United Kingdom at that time, it resurfaced in a form which could not be ignored in 1966.

Lloyd-Jones – one of the most senior and influential figures in British evangelicalism – had become increasingly anxious over the theological liberalism of the World Council of Churches. By 1965, he was convinced that it was impossible for an evangelical to belong to a denomination which was affiliated to the World Council of Churches. Evangelicals who were members of such churches would inevitably be 'contaminated' by others within these denominations who openly denied or challenged key elements of the Christian faith. Evangelicals who remained within doctrinally mixed churches – such as the Church of England – were therefore 'guilty by association' in that maintaining institutional links with liberals amounted to compromising their evangelical convictions.

In June 1965, Lloyd-Jones addressed the Westminster Fellowship, an interdenominational ministers' fraternal that met regularly in Westminster Chapel. Lloyd-Jones declared that theologically orthodox Anglicans and others should consider coming out of their 'contaminated' denominations.[21] Instead of believing that they could 'infiltrate the various bodies to which they belong and win them over' evangelicals should stand together outside the main denominations. Lloyd-Jones returned to this theme in December 1965 at the Puritan Studies Conference, declaring that attempts to reform a church from within had failed to take the New Testament doctrine of the Church seriously, putting expediency ahead of principles. There was only one solution: to join a doctrinally 'pure' denomination.

It was clear that a serious division was in the process of emerging, with Lloyd-Jones and Packer potentially on opposite sides of the divide. Anticipating this, Lloyd-Jones invited Packer to put the case for the continuing presence and involvement of evangelicals within the Church of England at a meeting of the Westminster Fellowship in March 1966. In the event, however, the expected confrontation between Lloyd-Jones and his critics centred on John Stott, not Packer.

On 18 October 1966, the National Assembly of Evangelicals brought together evangelicals from a wide variety of backgrounds at Central Hall, Westminster. Lloyd-Jones delivered the opening address to the Assembly. To the surprise of many, Lloyd-Jones adopted a mildly confrontational tone, arguing that evangelicals had failed to come to terms with the biblical doctrine of the Church: 'Ecumenical people put fellowship before doctrine. We, as evangelicals, put doctrine before fellowship.' Orthodox Christian believers who insisted on remaining in denominations 'tainted' by theological liberalism were, in effect, guilty of schism. They should leave and preserve their integrity. John Stott, who chaired this opening session, felt he had to intervene at this point, suggesting that the rightful and proper place of evangelicals may actually be *within* those mainstream denominations, which they might be able to renew from within.

Debate continues about precisely what Lloyd-Jones meant by his words, and whether Stott was right to intervene in this way. The religious press coverage of the occasion, however, seems to have crystallised wider perceptions of the events and their implications. The *Baptist Times* reported that Lloyd-Jones 'seemed to be encouraging evangelicals to secede from their denominations'. *The Christian* summarised Lloyd-Jones' speech under a banner headline

'Evangelicals – Leave your Denominations'. A major division now opened up within English evangelicalism over the specific issue of whether evangelicals had a defensible place within mainline British denominations, such as the Church of England.

That division extended to the Westminster Fellowship itself. At its next meeting on 28 November 1966 it became clear that there was a diversity of views over the issue of secession among those present. Lloyd-Jones declared that he believed the Fellowship had served its purpose, and should be disbanded.[22] It was subsequently reconstituted in such terms that those who believed that the mainline denominations could be reformed from within were excluded.[23] Ecclesiology, which had always been acknowledged as an issue over which evangelicals could disagree, had suddenly become a divisive and polarising thorn in British evangelicalism's side.

For Lloyd-Jones, it was inevitable that there would be 'a crisis on what is to me the fundamental issue, namely, do we believe in a territorial church or a gathered community of saints?'. It was far from clear that there need be such a crisis. The sixteenth-century Reformation had seen debate over precisely this issue, with Luther and Calvin adopting a territorial model, and the Anabaptists a 'gathered community of saints' model. It was well known that a close reading of the New Testament or a study of historical theology did not give a clear answer to this question, allowing most evangelicals to conclude that, while important to individual churches, this question could be seen as a secondary debate. Yet it was now being presented as a gospel issue, central to evangelical identity.

Where Lloyd-Jones proposed a vision of the Church as a 'gathered community of saints', Packer and Stott made the case for evangelicals seeing themselves as an *ecclesiola in ecclesia* – in other words, as a reforming body embedded within a state Church. Lloyd Jones and his colleagues argued for a 'pure body' doctrine of the Church, in which only those with explicitly evangelical convictions were to be accepted for membership. Packer conceded that his was the belief of mainstream Protestant Reformers, including both Martin Luther and John Calvin.

Packer developed and justified his views on the nature of the Church further in the course of the next decade. His fullest statement of his approach was set out in two pamphlets published by Latimer House, in which he notes the difficulties facing evangelicals in doctrinally mixed churches, such as the Church of England.[24] The arguments which Packer counters in these works are primarily those deriving from the circles around Lloyd-Jones, particularly the demand that evangelicals withdraw from such mixed churches to form 'pure' denominations:

> Some have urged evangelicals in 'doctrinally mixed' churches to withdraw into a tighter fellowship where the pre-critical, pre-liberal view of Scripture is rigorously upheld and sceptical revisionism in theology is debarred. It has been said that failure to do this is as unprincipled as it is foolish. It is unprincipled, the argument runs, because by staying in churches which tolerate heretics you become constructively guilty of their heresies, by your association with them; and it is foolish because you have not the least hope of cleaning up the Augean stables while liberals remain there. Withdrawal is the conscientious man's only option.[25]

Packer responded by noting that all mainstream churches are, as a matter of historical fact, founded on a set of beliefs (embodied in the Christian creeds and sets of confessional documents) which commits those churches to theological orthodoxy. Some may depart from this; evangelicals within those churches have a duty to recall them to faithfulness. They cannot be regarded as 'guilty by association' if they protest in this way. The very idea of 'guilt by association' was, for Packer, 'a nonsense notion, which has been given an unhappy airing during the last two decades'.[26] If trends towards liberalism are not resisted, a denomination will slide into heresy. And who will protest and argue against this, unless evangelicals remain within those mainline churches for as long as possible?

Packer also offered a criticism against those who argued that their own congregations or denominations were theologically correct. He noted that smaller doctrinally 'pure' bodies, such as the Federation of Independent Evangelical Churches, are open to the charge that they might 'purchase doctrinal purity at the price of theological stagnation, and are cultural backwaters out of touch with society around'.

Underlying this point is Packer's conviction that cultural engagement – of such importance to effective evangelism – is not assisted
by a total withdrawal from the society which is to be evangelised.

As a result of these serious disagreements about the nature of the
Church, the longstanding friendship between Lloyd-Jones and
Packer was now somewhat strained, though not yet irreparably
broken. Both had made public statements that showed that they held
opposed positions on a question which Lloyd-Jones had made of
defining importance for evangelicals. Packer held that evangelicals
within the Church of England must be free 'to pursue their historic
bilateral policy of fellowship with evangelicals in other denominations, and full involvement in their own church', and appealed to
writers such as George Whitefield, Charles Simeon and J. C. Ryle
in support of his position.

The National Evangelical Anglican Congress (1967)

It became clear that evangelical Anglicans needed to consider their
positions in the light of these developments. As it happened, plans
were already under way to convene a National Evangelical Anglican
Congress. These were now given a sense of urgency, as well as a
specific focus for discussion. The Congress was planned for April
1967 at the University of Keele. It was obvious that Latimer House
was strategically placed to resource the proposed event, so it became
its organisational and theological hub, including hosting a series of
meetings which led to the production of *Guidelines*, the collection of
essays which developed and defended the Keele agenda. These essays
showed how evangelicals within the Church of England could reas-
sert their presence within that Church over and against both liberal
Anglicans who wished to exclude them from membership, and some
Free Church evangelicals, loyal to Lloyd-Jones, who argued that they
had no business being members of that Church in the first place. As
Packer later remarked, 'Keele was the child of Latimer House.'

Yet even before the Congress of 1967, it was clear that Latimer
House was being seen as a core theological resource by younger
evangelical clergy of the Church of England. A conference on

'Facing the Future' held at Swanwick from 28 February to 2 March 1966 attracted two hundred such clergy, who called for a significant increase in Latimer House's funding to allow it to continue its work of identifying the issues which would confront the Church of England in the future. Perhaps most importantly, the conference asked Latimer House to convene Study Groups, focusing on these issues.[27] By January 1967, Packer and Beckwith had set in place plans for thirteen such groups. Philip A. Crowe was appointed as 'Study Groups Secretary', responsible for the coordination, administration and development of this new enterprise and by November 1967, in the aftermath of the National Evangelical Anglican Congress, the number of study groups had risen to fourteen, with 142 active members.[28]

The National Evangelical Anglican Congress took place in early April 1967 at Keele University in the north-west of England where a thousand people – 519 clergy and 481 laypeople – gathered for three days of intense debate and discussion of nine papers, charting possible ways ahead for evangelicalism within the Church of England. The papers included a significant reflection on 'Renewing the Local Church' by Packer's former colleague William Leathem, as well as Packer's own views on theological confessionalism. Delegates were assured that the purpose of the Congress was not just to 'beat old Evangelical drums, or shout old Evangelical slogans', but instead to 'grapple with live issues' and do 'some serious up-to-date thinking'. The nine conference addresses were designed to stimulate and unite, and appeared to have achieved their intended goals. For Packer, Keele brought evangelicals closer together, both intellectually and spiritually, and showcased conservative evangelicalism's vitality, energy and intellectual vigour.

While the Congress is rightly judged as a landmark in the history of Anglican evangelicalism, the nature of its legacy remains contested. At one level, it commended active engagement between evangelicals and the Church of England; at another, however, it created an uneasy tension between loyalty to the institution of the Church of England on the one hand, and a more profound loyalty to the gospel on the other.[29] Although the longer term ramifications of these tensions were perhaps overlooked in 1967, they have since led to significant fractures within both the Church of England and international Anglicanism. In 2002, Packer himself left the Anglican Church of Canada over issues of gender politics – something which nobody at Keele could have foreseen.

But what of Packer himself? Some thought that he would bask in the 'triumph of Keele' (that unfortunate superficial phrase was widely used at the time), which had seen Latimer House recognised as evangelical Anglicanism's theological 'think tank' and Packer as its premier theologian. But he realised that Latimer's role was changing. By 1968, he later reflected, Latimer House was in the process of becoming a networking facility, aiming to coordinate evangelical scholars, writers and activists around the country.[30] It was, Packer conceded, something that needed to be done. Yet he himself had other objectives: exploring the importance of theology for the life and ministry of the Church, for example, and developing resources that could help churches apply theology constructively and critically to their outreach and pastoral care. It was, he began to feel, an opportune moment to consider moving on.

Reflections on Possible Futures

What could Packer do next? Colin Brown, a member of staff at Tyndale Hall, Bristol, took the view that Packer ought to apply for a major British academic position – such as the Lady Margaret Chair of Divinity at Oxford, which became vacant in 1968 following the death of the patristic scholar Frank Leslie Cross. Packer, however, did not see a purely academic position like this as affirming his own understanding of his calling: 'I really am called, if I know anything at all, to make ministers and establish consciences, rather than to advance learning as an Oxbridge professor should.'[31]

Packer could also have taken up a position at a leading North American seminary. His growing international reputation would have made him an attractive proposition for a conservative evangelical seminary, such as Westminster Theological Seminary in Philadelphia or Trinity Evangelical Divinity School in Deerfield, Illinois. Rumours of this possibility were in circulation in England in

1968. John Wenham, a leading evangelical New Testament scholar who served as the Secretary to the Council of Latimer House, expressed alarm at the thought of such a move, given Packer's reputation and influence. British evangelicalism could not afford to lose him.

Wenham was right to believe that such a development was possible. Having spent some time in 1966 as a visiting professor at Westminster, and lectured at other seminaries in the Chicago area, Packer had noted approvingly how the ethos of American seminaries appeared to be determined more by the tone of their faculties than by their presidents.[33] The faculty were all treated as equals and were specialists in their fields. In contrast, Packer observed, the British equivalent of a seminary – the theological college – consisted of a Principal and a small number of members of staff, modelled on a vicar and his curates (a parish model), or a headmaster and his junior masters (a school model). Packer argued that this model was outdated.

In its place, Packer proposed 'some sort of parity pattern', in which the Principal of a theological college related to the members of staff like 'a faculty chairman in a university, or the leader of a team ministry of specialists'. In particular, Packer stressed the need to involve the teaching staff in the government of colleges, through direct staff representation on college governing bodies. Failure to do this would inevitably generate friction within the staff bodies.

Despite all this, Packer believed that he was called to serve in the British context, even if he was willing to spend time lecturing and teaching in North America. Rather than move to a North American seminary, he began to explore the idea of assuming a senior position in a theological college, and reshaping its structures in the light of their American equivalents. In June 1968, Packer informed the Latimer House Council that he was interested in pursuing the possibility of becoming the next Principal of the London College of Divinity, an evangelical theological college of the Church of England which had announced its decision to relocate to Nottingham in the East Midlands in the summer of 1970. The Governors of the College were looking for a dynamic and farsighted Principal to lead it as it entered a new phase. Packer figured that he might be able to offer the leadership they were seeking.

In the end, however, the Governors appointed the rising star Michael Green to the position. Green, who was already a member of staff at the College, had been the youngest of the plenary speakers at the Keele Congress, and was recognised as someone with significant leadership skills.[34] Green immediately invited Packer to take up the newly created position of Director of Studies at the college and Packer initially accepted the offer; after further reflection, though, he felt that this was probably not right and withdrew his acceptance.[35] Packer shared his uncertainties over his future with the Latimer House Council at its meeting in July 1969, and expressed the view that he ought to leave Latimer House at some point in 1970, even though at present there was no prospect of a new position elsewhere. While the Council was supportive of Packer, they naturally had to begin to consider potential replacements for him.[36]

But events were in motion elsewhere which would lead to Packer becoming Principal of Tyndale Hall, Bristol – the theological college at which he had taught with such distinction from 1954 to 1961. Although not realising it at the time, Packer was about to enter a phase of his ministry which boded well, yet would unexpectedly turn out to be one of the most stressful of his entire career.

We shall presently resume our narrative to tell the story of events in Bristol from 1968 to 1971, and how these shaped the direction of Packer's work. But first, we must turn to a theme which has been significant throughout Packer's career, and would be an important consideration in leading to his appointment as Principal of Tyndale Hall – the role of theology in the life of the Church.

8

Theology and the Life of the Church

Packer's constant emphasis on the importance of theology in the life of the Church contrasted with the more pragmatic techniques that had gained the ascendancy in British theological education since the First World War. Those preparing for ministry in the churches went to theological colleges for training, often being taught basic pastoral skills by clergy who either took a few years out from their ministry to teach full-time at these colleges, or who would spend several hours a week with those in training, discussing how best to preach or minister. It was an inherited model of training for ministry that had served the Church well in the past. But would it continue to work in the future?

Packer thought not. It was a purely pragmatic model of ministerial training, which emphasised the acquisition of certain techniques (such as pastoral care and preaching) and of a body of knowledge (mainly aspects of the professional culture of the Church of England, within which they would work). This is not a criticism of the Church of England: such models of theological education were commonplace at the time. Packer, however, was convinced that good preaching and pastoral practice emerged from good theology, which was the fundamental resource on which Christian ministry was ultimately based. What was required was the coordination of theology and the life of faith – a vision which Packer found in the preaching, pastoral practices and spiritual disciplines of the Puritans.

There were, of course, institutions of theological education beyond England which recognised the importance of the integration of theology and ministry. New College, Edinburgh, was one of the most important institutions of theological education in the Church of Scotland. Thomas F. Torrance served as its Professor of Christian

Dogmatics from 1952 to 1979, and stressed the importance of theology for ministry. Having himself served in the pastoral ministry of the Church of Scotland from 1940 to 1950, Torrance had given much thought to the integration of the Christian mind and Christian ministerial practice, finding the theology of Karl Barth particularly helpful in this enterprise.[1] Many larger American seminaries – Princeton Theological Seminary and Fuller Theological Seminary, for instance – had faculty members specialising in the field of practical theology.

An authentic Christian theology can never be an abstract intellectual pursuit, disengaged from the Christian life or the Church. While Warden of Latimer House, Packer made it clear that he did not wish to conduct what he perhaps unfairly dismissed as 'ivory tower theology'; his commitment was to a theology that was attentive to the pastoral, homiletic and spiritual ministry of the Church. Although it is fair to object that some of the world's leading academic theologians of that day – such as Torrance himself – shared Packer's concern to integrate theology with the Christian life, Packer's point needs to be taken seriously. It is fatally easy for theology to become the abstract and detached study of other theologians, rather than a principled and intentional commitment to enrich and inform the individual and communal life of faith.

Some of Packer's published pieces are intellectually outstanding, showing a range and depth of theological knowledge, linked with the ability to offer both critical analysis and constructive synthesis.[2] Packer could easily have written substantial academic monographs that would have graced the catalogues of the world's leading university presses – Cambridge, Chicago, Harvard, Oxford, Princeton or Yale. Yet he chose not to. Packer had no doubt what his intended readership was, and developed such a sustained and committed relationship with this readership over a period of fifty years that he became the 'go to' theologian for evangelicals, especially from a Reformed perspective, wanting an authentic, and accessible exploration of the Christian faith, particularly since his work tended to focus on nurturing the Christian life of his individual readers. Packer's repeated emphasis on the importance of catechesis and spirituality resonated well with this readership, especially in the United States.

The Italian political theorist Antonio Gramsci makes a helpful point here in his concept of an 'organic intellectual'.[3] Gramsci refers to thinkers whose authority does not rise from imposition, but who rather gather a following on account of their capacity to speak to the needs and situations of individuals and communities. We could think of Packer as an 'organic theologian' – someone whose standing and influence are the natural outcome of the respect in which he is held within a specific community, which recognises that he takes their hopes, fears and needs seriously, and that he is able to address them in a manner that is both trustworthy and approachable. Gramsci suggests that communities seek and find authority in trusted and wise individuals – whether or not they have been accredited by the academy. Packer's proven record of fidelity to the Christian tradition, his love for the gospel and responsible, informed endeavours to relate faith to life are all clearly acknowledged and appreciated by his many readers.

Many have argued that theological education in the United States and Britain during the nineteenth century was based on the fundamental assumption of the mutual interconnectedness of theology, spirituality and ministry.[4] Yet much of Packer's theological reflection took place during a later period in Western culture which saw the 'fragmentation' of Christian theology. In his notable study *Theologia: The Fragmentation and Unity of Theological Education* (1983), Edward Farley identified a series of developments in post-war theological education which led to the loss of a defining theological vision characterised by the 'coinherence of piety and intellect'.[5] Farley argues that the term *theologia* has lost its original meaning, which he defines as 'sapiential and personal knowledge of divine self-disclosure' leading to 'wisdom or discerning judgement indispensable for human living'. Theology used to be – and, in Farley's view, still could and should be – 'not just objective science, but a personal knowledge of God and the things of God'.

It is instructive to read Packer's substantial publishing output with these issues in mind, particularly the sundering of the link between piety and intellect. Farley's plea for a reconnection of what we might call a 'discipleship of the heart' and a 'discipleship of the mind' is echoed and treated in many of Packer's writings, especially those which emphasise the quintessential interconnection of theology and spirituality.[6] Packer, however, did not formulate his vision of theology in response to this fragmentation, as if his theology was an attempt to put things back together again; he works with a vision of theology which affirms the fundamental integration of the reasonable and experiential, the theoretical and practical, from the outset.

Packer argues that it is never enough for us to *know about* God; true Christian theology is about *knowing* God – a relational and transformative process of knowing and being known, which sustains and informs the Christian life. The Christian encounter with God is transformative. As Packer, following Calvin, pointed out, to know God is to be changed by God; true knowledge of God leads to worship, as the believer is caught up in a transforming and renewing encounter with the living God. The ultimate test of whether we have grasped theological truth is thus not so much whether we have comprehended it rationally, but whether it has transformed us experientially. In an important sense, we are not called on to master theology, but to allow it to master us. This helps us understand Packer's intense concern with Christian piety, especially as this is expressed and sustained by the doctrine of sanctification.[7]

At one level, Packer regards theology as informative – that is to say, disclosing to us the way things really are; or inviting us to think and talk about God and the created order in the light of God's own self-disclosure in history and Scripture. The proper subject matter of systematic theology is revealed truth about the works, ways and will of God, which is developed exegetically through an engagement with Scripture and 'brought together in a single coherent scheme'.[8] Theology weaves together biblical threads, engendering a grander vision of things to be discerned. Theology thus provides a biblically grounded and intellectually coherent account of God, our world and ourselves, allowing us rightly to discern the character and wisdom of God, together with our true identity, natural capacities and ultimate destiny. For this reason, there is an intimate link between theology and worship, as we respond in delight, awe and humility to the reality of God that theology discloses: 'We are called to make our study of theology a devotional discipline, a verifying in experience of

Aquinas' beautiful remark that theology is taught by God, teaches God, and takes us to God.'[9] ok ~ good

Theology tells us the truth about God and ourselves, whether we like what we are told or not. We must thus be prepared to face up to the challenging view of human nature and capacities that is embedded within the Christian faith, and respond accordingly. Yet Packer sees such insights as liberating, rather than discouraging – especially in dealing with the problem of 'indwelling sin'. Packer, who knew such unease and anxiety over this issue himself, provides both an accurate description of this phenomenon, and what he considers to be a reliable prescription for its remedy. Christians, he suggests, 'will live in tension and distress at their frustrating infirmities'. They are disheartened, in that they keep 'discerning sinful desires in themselves despite their longing to be sin-free'.[10] What they yearn for seems to lie tantalisingly beyond their grasp.

What, then, can be done about this? Packer often answers this question by drawing on his own experience as a young convert to Christianity at Oxford, who realised that the sin that formerly dominated him 'had been de-throned but was not yet destroyed'.[11] Sin was 'marauding within me all the time, bringing back sinful desires that I hoped I had seen the last of, and twisting my new desires for God and godliness out of shape'. Grace might subdue sin, yet it does not wholly remove it. We are to 'put on' Christ, as we might put on a garment, which leads to 'an implanting in us of the inclinations of Christ's perfect humanity through our ingrafting into him', which in turn produces within us 'a mind-set and lifestyle that is not explicable in terms of what we were before'.[12] We are called to be watchful, and to fight against sin. Sanctification is indeed enabled by God – yet it demands an ongoing, determined struggle in faith. God works in and through the Christian's efforts to bring about transformation and renewal.[13]

How, we might ask, does theology impact on the life of the Church? Packer tends to concentrate on the difference that theology makes to individuals, particularly in helping them to develop their own personal piety. Yet his theology of the Church highlights the corporate aspects of the life of faith, making it clear that an individual's growth in piety is located within and enriched by the community of faith. Christians can be thought of as 'a little flock in a largely hostile environment', who often struggle in the face of such enmity and isolation.[14] Packer emphasises the need for 'mutual love and care in God's family on the basis that this is the life to which we are called and for which Christ equips us'.[15] While individualism may come naturally to us, it can be unhealthy; it often represents a 'proud unwillingness to accept a place in a team of peers and to be bound by group consensus'. For this reason, Packer insists on distinguishing between *individualism* and *individuality*. Being a Christian ripens and extends our individuality; individualism, however, is a form of sin. ? Not sure

So what about doctrines that many Christians find challenging to believe? A good example is the doctrine of the Trinity, which many ordinary believers find intellectually puzzling and spiritually irrelevant. Where some theologians set out to offer a reasoned defence of this doctrine, Packer prefers to adopt a more traditional evangelical approach, reaffirming its roots in the Bible. In his *Concise Theology*, Packer argues that the biblical witness to the 'one God, the self-revealed Creator' is that this one God is portrayed in the New Testament as 'three personal agents, Father, Son, and Holy Spirit, working together in the manner of a team to bring about salvation'.[16] The doctrine of the Trinity is the Church's appropriate response to this mystery, aiming to safeguard and preserve it – not to explain it.

Accepting that the doctrine of the Trinity is not *explicitly* formulated in the New Testament, Packer nevertheless notes that its basic themes are unquestionably present: 'Though the technical language of historic trinitarianism is not found there, trinitarian faith and thinking are present throughout its pages, and in that sense the Trinity must be acknowledged as a biblical doctrine.' It is clear that Packer's comments are here intended for an intelligent lay audience as his conclusion concerning the practical implications of this doctrine would indicate: 'The practical importance of the doctrine of the Trinity is that it requires us to pay equal attention, and give equal honor, to all three persons in the unity of their gracious ministry to us.'

Yet in an explicitly academic context, Packer offers a more nuanced and intricate account of the doctrine, highlighting the similarities between his own thinking on this matter and that of the Scottish theologian James Orr.[17] Packer here stresses that the Church's doctrine of the Trinity arose essentially from intense reflection on the identity and significance of Jesus Christ. Orr realised that the truth of the Trinity was 'the first of the corollaries of the doctrine of the Incarnation', thus displaying his awareness that 'Christian trinitarianism is essentially an affirmation about Jesus Christ'. Packer approvingly cites Orr's defence of a trinitarian faith:

> The doctrine of the Trinity is not a result of mere speculation . . . still less, as some eminent writers would maintain, the result of the importation of Greek metaphysics into Christian theology. It is, in the first instance, the result of a simple process of induction from the facts of the Christian Revelation.[18] OK ~ I John 5:7 K JV

For Packer, Orr's recovery of the doctrine of the Trinity has been consolidated by orthodox Christian theology since the Second World War, noting particularly the contributions of Robert Jenson, Thomas F. Torrance, Colin Gunton, Millard Erickson, Jürgen Moltmann and Wolfhart Pannenberg. As a result, there is now a 'renewed awareness' that a 'consistent and thoroughgoing Trinitarianism' is basic to authentic Christian evangelism, nurture and pastoral care, all 'leading into the life of prayer, purity, and praise, which is our true spiritual health'.

It is clear that, when all is said and done, Packer's vision of what theology ought to *be* – and what theologians ought to *do* – remains anchored to the Puritan tradition, which both affirmed and employed an 'experimental theology' to illuminate and engage the realities of the spiritual life. While Packer ranges far more widely than Puritanism in his theological explorations, he constantly returns to Puritan writers as exemplars of theologians who were committed to the Church and to strengthening the life of faith.

Packer's vision of the purpose and place of theology also has institutional implications. The proper location for the study of theology is not the dispassionate and disinterested world of the academy, but the committed world of the community of faith. Packer's aspiration for a theological college of the Church of England was that it would affirm the fundamental coinherence of biblical studies, theology, pastoral care and piety – and thus equip future clergy to develop their own spiritual lives, as well as those committed to their care.

In practice, however, most British theological colleges of the 1960s saw these as autonomous disciplines. All had to be taught to meet the formal requirements for ordination; they were not, however, regarded as interconnected components of a greater whole. Packer would, as we shall see, attempt to implement his coherent scheme of theology when he became Principal of Tyndale Hall, Bristol. Yet perhaps more importantly, one of the factors that drew Packer to Regent College, Vancouver, was encountering precisely this integrated vision of Christian theology in action.

We now take up our narrative once again, as Packer prepared to return to Bristol in a new leadership role which would allow him to reshape the theological education of future ministers.

9

A New Beginning? Trinity College, Bristol

On 4 August 1969, it was announced that Packer would become the Principal of Tyndale Hall, Bristol. It was a good appointment, which was widely welcomed within the evangelical constituency, allowing Packer to use his talents to good effect. Yet Packer's optimism about his future quickly evaporated, as the future of theological education at Bristol – especially at Tyndale Hall – was called into question by a series of decisions made by the Church of England in early 1971 about the direction of ministerial training. Given the importance of this difficult period for Packer, we need to look at these developments in Bristol in some detail.

Tensions at Bristol: Clifton Theological College and Tyndale Hall

In the summer of 1969, the Church of England had two accredited evangelical theological colleges in Bristol, namely, Clifton Theological College and Tyndale Hall, both of which had connections with the Bible Churchmen's Missionary Society. The relationship between the two colleges was not easy, in that the origins of Clifton lay in a serious rift between the staff of Tyndale Hall and the Bible Churchmen's Missionary Society back in the 1930s. As the memories of this split faded into history, the question of why there should be two evangelical theological colleges so close together in Bristol began to be raised. Surely there was a case for a merger? Two senior members of staff at each institution – John Wenham at Tyndale and Alec Motyer at Clifton – had been talking about the case for a merger since 1960.

Any hope of the reunification of Bristol's two theological colleges was dashed, however, by a series of events in February 1965. A serious dispute between the Principal of Clifton Theological College and his teaching staff led to three of the five members of staff being summoned before the College Council late at night and summarily dismissed. Two other staff members resigned in sympathy shortly afterwards. These events caused consternation and distress far beyond Clifton, particularly at Tyndale Hall. Most of the staff there had good professional and personal relationships with their colleagues at Clifton and were shocked at the dismissals. Colin Brown, a member of the Tyndale staff, publicly criticised the developments at Clifton in a paper set before the Church of England Theological Council. It was inevitable that institutional relationships between Clifton and Tyndale would become severely impaired.

Nonetheless, news of this rift did not filter through to the senior echelons of the national Church. In February 1968, the Church of England published a report entitled *Theological Colleges for Tomorrow*. Its most striking recommendation was that theological colleges should have an optimum size of 120, and a minimum of eighty. The creation of institutions of this size could only be achieved by mergers between existing ones. The report's main author, Sir Bernard de Bunsen, seems to have assumed that, as Clifton and Tyndale were both evangelical colleges located in the same area of Bristol, a merger between them was natural and unproblematic.

A joint meeting of the teaching staff of both institutions to discuss this possibility was arranged for 18 June 1968. Tensions between the two staff bodies flared up, leading the Tyndale staff to request that negotiations should cease. The College Councils, who acted as trustees for the institutions, saw no reason to take these conflicts into account, and agreed to work towards a merger. The decision was announced to both College communities in October 1968. It was very badly received at Tyndale, especially when it became clear that the merger plan included an explicit decision not to appoint Colin Brown to the staff of the new College, on account of his criticism of the dismissal of staff at Clifton in 1965.

On 18 October 1968, a 'declaration of intent' to unite the two Colleges by September 1970 under the leadership of a new Principal,

Michael Baughen, was jointly issued by the two College Councils. Yet Packer had not been considered by the College Councils as a potential Principal of the new college. There was growing discontent on the part of staff and students alike at Tyndale Hall over the conspicuous absence of a person of scholarly or theological distinction on the proposed staff of the new College.

In the end, the final blow to the merger came from the Bible Churchmen's Missionary Society, who had a continuing interest in the governance of Tyndale Hall. Aware of the growing criticism of the merger from within their constituency, they resolved at an extraordinary meeting in May 1969 not to support it. Without that support, the merger could not – and did not – proceed.[1]

The plans for a merged College were now unworkable. What, then, would happen to Tyndale Hall? Could it survive on its own? The future seemed highly uncertain. Perhaps inevitably, the Principal of Tyndale Hall announced his resignation following the failure of the merger negotiations, with effect from the end of December 1969. Tyndale now needed a new Principal. Student enrolments had fallen sharply as a result of concerns about the merger negotiations within the College's core constituency. The parlous state of the College was evident: only twenty-eight students had been enrolled for the academic year 1969–70. The financial situation was serious, with significant losses being predicted. There was an urgent need for Tyndale Hall to reconnect with its support base, by appointing a Principal who commanded respect within that group, and who possessed the theological competency that staff as well as students regarded as essential to the College's future.

On 21 July 1969, Packer was invited to a meeting of the Council, and spent two hours in general discussion, addressing a series of specific questions put to him by Council members. Although there were other applications, the Council clearly felt that Packer was the right man for the job. They did not waste time in letting the General Committee of the Bible Churchmen's Missionary Society know the identity of the various applicants, as well as their belief that Packer was the obvious choice as Principal. When the Committee met the following day they warmly endorsed the invitation. On 4 August, the outgoing Principal of Tyndale Hall was able to write to students, confirming that Packer would be his successor, and that all current full-time teaching staff, including Colin Brown, would remain in their positions.

A Reforming Principal: Changes at Tyndale Hall

Packer would be a reforming Principal, alert to the need to restore the reputation of the College within its constituency, as well as to refresh the structures and curriculum of the College itself. Packer's first objective was to review and reform the governance of Tyndale Hall, and eliminate as much of its traditional paternalism as possible; his second was to establish an outstanding faculty whose reputation would attract students to the College. Packer got to work on both these matters before he formally took up the Principalship of Tyndale Hall on 1 January 1970. First, he set up a working party to oversee the revision of the government of Tyndale Hall. At its first meeting in October 1969, Packer announced that he had appointed Alec Motyer as lecturer in Old Testament. Motyer, who had been Vice-Principal of Clifton Theological College until the 'events of 1965', was at that time serving in parish ministry at St Luke's, Hampstead, in London. The appointment was well received by the student body, and helped boost Tyndale's profile and appeal.[2] The working party met for a second time from 31 October to 1 November 1969, aiming to identify key objectives for the College, and plan its internal restructuring to ensure a sense of partnership and ownership across the Council, staff and students. Three main changes were proposed.

First, a new body, the 'Tyndale Hall Association', would be created with responsibility for administering the College. Its membership would be by subscription. One quarter of the College Council would be elected directly by Association members. In this way, Packer believed that the College would remain sensitive and responsive to the concerns of its supporters, and be able to resist centralising and standardising pressures from Church authorities.

Second, all full-time teaching staff would serve on the Hall Council *ex officio*, ensuring that the serious communication break-down between Council and staff of 1968 would never happen again.

And, third, the College syllabus and pastoral training programme would be reviewed to ensure that it met the needs of the Church, while retaining Tyndale's distinctive emphasis on the importance of theology.

Having been involved in planning for the College's future throughout the second half of 1969, Packer formally took up his position as Principal on 1 January 1970. He presided over what was recognised at the time as an outstanding group of colleagues: Alec Motyer (Deputy Principal, with teaching responsibilities in Hebrew and Old Testament); Colin Brown (Dean of Studies, with teaching responsibilities in church history, historical theology, and the philosophy of religion); Anthony Thiselton (teaching responsibilities in New Testament theology, biblical interpretation and the philosophy of religion); and John Tiller (teaching responsibilities in the area of worship and church history). No English theological college, before or after, has ever managed to pack in quite so great a concentration of theological talent. There was every confidence that Tyndale had a vibrant future ahead of it, now that the difficulties of the last few years had been laid to rest. All that was needed was time to allow things to settle down, and to enable Tyndale's new vision to become more widely known and appreciated within the English Church.

Yet Packer had hardly settled in to his new position when ominous storm clouds began to gather on the horizon. Tyndale's future was unexpectedly called into question again. And to make things even worse, Packer's longstanding and increasingly brittle friendship with Dr Martyn Lloyd-Jones came under new stress, and finally ruptured.

Martyn Lloyd-Jones: The Parting of the Ways

In his final report of October 1969 to the Latimer House Council, Packer mentioned a number of projects which were now coming to completion, including a short work entitled *Growing into Union*. Its four authors were Graham Leonard, E. L. Mascall, Colin O. Buchanan and Packer. Buchanan and Packer were evangelicals; Leonard and Mascall were leading Anglo-Catholics (that is to say, members of the catholic wing of the Church of England). Packer would later comment on the 'happy fact' that within the last few decades, the previously felt 'convictional and kerygmatic gap' between conservative evangelical Anglicans and conservative Anglo-Catholics had shrunk.

At this time, however, it was highly unusual for evangelicals and Anglo-Catholics to collaborate on such projects. Packer nevertheless felt that it was necessary for evangelicals and Anglo-Catholics who were theologically orthodox to challenge the liberal ideology that seemed to lie behind proposals for a union between the Church of England and Methodists in England. Packer and his three colleagues stressed the importance of theology, and especially the need for theological *orthodoxy*, in any plans for a church union. It was a strategy that Packer believed was essential in the light of a rising tide of liberalism within the English churches – namely, affirming common ground between evangelicals and Anglo-Catholics within the Church of England, while noting genuine points of disagreement over other issues – such as the authority of the Bible or the nature of sacraments.

Growing into Union was published in May 1970. It received strongly negative reviews from many traditionalist Protestants, such as David Samuel of the Protestant Reformation Society. The most important and damaging criticisms, however, were voiced by Martin Lloyd-Jones and his circle. For Lloyd-Jones, the book represented a compromise, brought about through a weakening of evangelical convictions. Lloyd-Jones, supported by John Caiger and David Fountain (the other Free Church members of the Puritan Conference Committee), wrote to Packer to terminate the Puritan Conferences. In the circumstances, they believed, it was impossible for them to continue – despite Packer's crucial role in founding those Conferences. A meeting of the Westminster Fraternal in November 1970 requested that the Conference should be reconvened in an appropriately modified form in the following year, under the new title of the 'Westminster Conference'.

Packer now found himself being shunned by evangelical organisations which would once have counted him as their friend and ally, with some even suggesting that Packer could 'no longer be regarded as an evangelical'. Arrogant and misguided though this judgement now seems, it reflected the hardening views now settling in within the Lloyd-Jones camp, which decided to take an absolute stand over what was actually a secondary issue.

This public rejection of Packer by the Lloyd-Jones contigent was painful for Packer, not least on account of the very high esteem in which he held Lloyd-Jones. It was little comfort that the strategy proved abortive. Without the cachet afforded them by Packer's reputation, many of the bodies who had frozen him out found themselves lacking figures of substance to support them. Packer had been one of the relatively few influential evangelicals within the Church of England to champion links with Lloyd-Jones. With that connection so publicly broken by Lloyd-Jones himself, the scene was set for the further marginalisation of his influence within the English national Church in general, and evangelical Anglicanism in particular.

Although this termination of an important friendship was distressing, Packer soon discovered that he had other things to worry about. By the end of 1970, the future of Tyndale Hall itself was thrown into serious doubt. Having just emerged from one crisis, Tyndale now found itself plunged into another.

A New Crisis: The End of Tyndale Hall?

To understand the crisis that overtook Tyndale Hall, we need to reflect on the changing fortunes of theological education in the Church of England during the 1960s. The decade opened with the Church of England in a buoyant mood. From 1961 to 1964, ordinations exceeded six hundred a year for the first time since before the First World War, and there was a widespread expectation that these numbers would rise still further. In an influential report of 1964, the sociologist Leslie Paul optimistically – and, as it turned out, wrongly – predicted that there would be more than eight hundred ordinations a year by the 1970s.[3]

By the late 1960s, however, the surge in ordinand numbers faltered, and then declined. There was no way in which all of the Church of England's existing theological colleges could survive, given this unexpected and serious decline in students. Some began to run at a loss, and faced the threat of bankruptcy, including Wycliffe Hall, Oxford, where Packer himself had trained for ministry.[4] A significant reorganisation of theological education within the Church of England was necessary to cope with this unforeseen reversal in the number of students who felt called to ministry. The de Bunsen report of February 1968 led to the formation of a Joint Planning Group, which outlined two possible strategies for the future: allowing the present situation to continue, so that student numbers would be determined by market forces; or making a centralised decision concerning the future of individual theological colleges.

In February 1970, the Church Assembly debated the future of theological education, aware of falling numbers of candidates for ordination. Although the debate raised wide-ranging questions, there was no doubt about its outcome: decisions over the future of individual theological colleges would be taken centrally. Some colleges would be merged; others would be closed. In April 1970, Packer reported that it was now expected that the number of theological colleges would be reduced from twenty-one to fourteen. One in three colleges would cease to exist in their present form. The threat to Tyndale was evident: student numbers were low, the College was facing a deficit for the year 1969–70, and another was projected for 1970–1. Its economic viability was open to question and it could not continue on its own. Closure or merger seemed inevitable.[5]

Six of the seven evangelical theological college councils decided to set up a working party to explore their options, chaired by John Stott. On 25 September, Stott and his colleagues issued their report. There seemed to be only two viable solutions for the situation in Bristol: a merger between Clifton, Tyndale and Dalton House; or a merger of Clifton with Wycliffe Hall, Oxford; and of Tyndale with Dalton House. The group, however, noted that the removal of Clifton would probably lead to the demise of Tyndale Hall, and hence the ending of any evangelical theological presence in Bristol. The group therefore suggested that the most realistic option was for a merger of the three Bristol Colleges.

Important though this report was, it was purely unofficial, and carried no weight within the Church of England. The official

Commission, chaired by Robert A. K. Runcie (Bishop of St Albans, later Archbishop of Canterbury), recommended that theological training should cease in Bristol altogether. Clifton was directed to move to Oxford, where it would merge with Wycliffe Hall; Tyndale was directed to move to Nottingham, where it would merge with the relocating London College of Divinity (which would be known as 'St John's College, Nottingham'). There would be no remaining theological colleges in Bristol. The Commission made it clear that it had given careful consideration to a possible merger between Clifton and Tyndale in Bristol, but had been advised that it stood little chance of success: 'We cannot help being impressed by the Faculty which is being assembled at Tyndale Hall, and the new curriculum which is being worked out, but we believe that they would be of better service to the church if they combined with St John's to form a strong united college at Nottingham.'

The proposal to end theological training in Bristol came as a thunderbolt from the blue to both Tyndale and Clifton. The Tyndale Hall Council, meeting the following day, decided to write immediately to St John's College, Nottingham, to sound them out over the recommendation that they should merge. The resulting consultation between representatives of Clifton, Tyndale, Wycliffe and St John's led to a consensus that an Anglican evangelical theological college should remain in Bristol, in that the suggestion that Tyndale should move to Nottingham was impractical.

The final decision, however, rested with the bishops of the Church of England. After due consideration, they announced their decision in February 1971. The outcome was bleak for Tyndale Hall. The bishops had decided that Tyndale was to be closed with effect from 1 October 1971. Three other colleges were also earmarked for closure; however, in each case, it was proposed that they be reopened in the future if student numbers increased. No such provision was made for Tyndale. The bishops endorsed the recommendation of the Runcie Commission that Clifton should merge with Wycliffe Hall on the Oxford site.

The Bishop of Bristol, Oliver Tomkins, however, objected to the ending of Anglican theological education in the south-west of England. He urged reconsideration of the decision, arguing for a theological college to remain in Bristol, despite his own theological differences with evangelicalism. As a result of Tomkins' vigorous last-minute lobbying, the bishops announced a significant revision of their earlier recommendation a few weeks later:

> In the opinion of the House of Bishops, the continuation of train-ing for ordinands at Bristol is only possible if Tyndale Hall, Clifton and Dalton St Michael's agree to amalgamate on the Clifton site . . . The House, therefore, asks that the Governing Bodies of the colleges concerned should immediately explore this possibility and submit their decisions to the House of Bishops not later than 1 May 1971.

Oliver Tomkins wasted no time in getting this process under way. He immediately wrote to Packer and the Principals of Clifton and Dalton, informing them that he would be prepared to chair the joint meeting which would negotiate a merger between them, on condi-tion that all members of staff and governors submitted their resigna-tions, to allow for a new college to be formed. Not all those currently involved with the three existing Colleges could expect to serve the new institution. This unsettling precondition was nevertheless agreed, and negotiations for the creation of a new theological college in Bristol began.

The Creation of Trinity College, Bristol

There was unequivocal agreement on the relatively simple matter that the new institution should be named 'Trinity College'. Other affairs, however, took longer to resolve. The financial basis of the merged College was more or less settled, as was the question of its doctrinal ethos. The leadership was conceived as a triumvirate of three senior staff: a Dean of College, a Dean of Studies and a Dean of Women. The working group made it clear that it had specific individuals in mind for each of these positions: an existing member of the Clifton staff was mentioned in connection with the first; Packer in connection with the second; and Joyce Baldwin (Dalton) in connection with the third. No mention was made of a single Principal with overall charge of the institution. In addition to the three deans, there would be three other teaching staff members. The House of Bishops met on 11 May and gave broad approval to the proposals; yet discussion continued, as some Clifton representatives believed it was essential that the new Trinity College should have a Principal, not merely a senior management team.

On 6 October, agreement was announced. The Church of England would recognise a new united theological college at Bristol, with Alec Motyer, a former colleague of Packer's at Tyndale Hall, as Principal. Packer would become Associate Principal, with a brief to develop theological education and maintain links with similar institutions in England and overseas. This gave him a major role in the future direction of the College, while allowing him time for writing and research. No members of staff of any of the three Colleges would be made redundant as a result of the merger. Joint teaching between the three Colleges would begin in October, and operations would move entirely to the Clifton site with effect from 1 January 1972. The combined College would have about eighty students and hopes were high that this would grow over time.

With the completion of the merger negotiations between the three Bristol Colleges, a period of relative calm settled over Packer and his Bristol colleagues. While the practical preparations to merge the three Colleges into a single unit proved to be challenging, if not exhausting, theological education in Bristol was no longer under any threat. By the middle of 1972, a degree of normality had been restored. Trinity College had come into being and was attracting students. There was no longer any need to worry unduly about the future, at least in the short term.

Under Motyer's leadership, much of the vision for theological education which had emerged at Tyndale Hall under Packer was carried over into the new united College. For many young evangelicals, Packer and Motyer together represented a form of evangelicalism which possessed both intellectual rigour and spiritual integrity. Under their joint leadership, Trinity College began to attract more students than before from college and university Christian Unions. Prospects seemed secure.

While Packer was no longer Principal of a theological college, his new situation gave him more time to read, think and write. Freed from much of the crippling burden of administration which is the inevitable lot of a theological college Principal in England, Packer was free to begin to start writing and thinking again. He had been under more or less continuous pressure from 1970 to 1972, making it difficult for him to undertake major research or writing projects. As Trinity settled down, Packer again found he had time and space for thinking, speaking and writing. He was able to develop a link with St Edyth's Church, Sea Mills, a local Anglican parish, which helped Packer embed his theology in a pastoral context.

Perhaps more significantly, Packer was able to negotiate an arrangement with the College Council to allow him to spend the autumn and spring terms focusing on his teaching in Bristol, leaving the summer term free of commitments so he could spend time in North America. Packer's North American tours, which would last up to ten weeks at a time, enabled him to develop personal contacts and his theological horizons. Increasingly, Packer became a well-known figure in North America – not simply through his books, but through his personal presence at seminaries as a teacher and lecturer.

One of the books which resulted from Packer's new situation would gain him a substantial international reputation, far beyond any he had known in the past. The book? *Knowing God.*

IO

Theology and Spirituality: *Knowing God*

During the 1950s, a series of individuals came to faith through the ministry of Westminster Chapel, London. One such convert was Elizabeth Braund, a journalist then working with the British Broadcasting Corporation. It seemed natural to Lloyd-Jones to encourage Braund to put her obvious talents to Christian service. The result was the *Evangelical Magazine*, which initially had Braund as its managing editor. Lloyd-Jones invited Packer and J. Elwyn Davies to serve as consulting editors.

Elwyn Davies was then Secretary of the Evangelical Movement of Wales, and had been involved in creating and producing the Welsh-language publication *Y Cylchgrawn Efengylaidd* (*The Evangelical Magazine*). His experience would be invaluable in getting the new publication off the ground. In June 1959, the three editors issued a circular letter announcing that the new publication would appear for the first time in September 1959, and emphasising that the new magazine would not be 'identified with any particular groups or interests, denominational or otherwise'. It was expected that the magazine would have six editions each year. It soon reached a circulation of about three thousand.

Packer's involvement with this journal is an excellent example of the 'bilateral' policy he had consistently followed, which allowed him to work together with evangelicals across denominational lines, while at the same time affirming his commitment to and involvement in the life and ministry of the Church of England. Braund invited Packer to write a series of articles on the general theme of 'God', aimed at a readership which was 'fed up with religious verbiage', who were prepared to do some honest and serious thinking, and 'want reality'. Packer mulled this over and agreed to produce a regular series of about five articles a year on knowing God in the believer's mind, heart and life.

Earlier, we noted the breakdown in relationships between Packer and Lloyd-Jones following the publication of Packer's edited volume *Growing into Union* in May 1970 (see pp. 93–4). Packer now found himself frozen out of Lloyd-Jones's circle. Braund and Elwyn Davies were close to Lloyd-Jones, perhaps making it inevitable that he would be thrown off the Editorial Board of the *Evangelical Magazine*. It was, of course, equally inevitable that, deprived of its star writer, the magazine would have little appeal. It folded shortly afterwards. The original Welsh-language magazine *Y Cylchgrawn Efengylaidd*, in contrast, continues to this day.

Packer now wondered what to do with his series of articles on God. One obvious possibility was suggested by C. S. Lewis's well-known work *The Screwtape Letters*, which originally took the form of a series of pieces in a Christian magazine. At that time, Packer was preoccupied with preparing to move from Latimer House, Oxford, to take up the Principalship of Tyndale Hall, Bristol, and had little opportunity to develop the articles into a book. In any case, Inter-Varsity Fellowship did not seem interested in a book from Packer on this topic. Ronald Inchley, who had published Packer's two earlier works *'Fundamentalism' and the Word of God* and *Evangelism and the Sovereignty of God* made it clear that he was very happy to work with Packer on another book – provided it dealt with the charismatic movement, which Inchley rightly saw as growing in importance within evangelical circles. In the end, Packer obliged: *Keep in Step with the Spirit* appeared in 1984.

Yet Packer realised there was another possibility. During the 1960s, the Church of England Evangelical Council, under its Chairman John Stott, recognised the need for a series of accessible books addressing contemporary topics of relevance. It was agreed that the series would have the running title *Christian Foundations*, and would consist of individual volumes that were to be 20,000 words in length, to be produced at two-monthly intervals and extending over a period of several years.[1] The series would be published by Hodder & Stoughton, a mainline London publishing house with extensive interests in the fiction and reference markets, as well as a long tradition of publishing significant Christian works. Stott, Michael Green and Packer were among the first authors to be invited to contribute to the series. Packer's concise and accessible ninety-six-page volume entitled *God has Spoken* (1965) dealt with the issue of biblical inspiration and the nature of revelation.

Packer could easily see the merits of offering Hodder & Stoughton the book he had in mind, and travelled to London to visit Edward England, who by then had established a reputation as a canny commissioning editor. Although some in Hodder & Stoughton wanted to end the company's commitment to Christian publishing in the early 1960s, England's publishing successes put an end to any such ideas. Shortly after his arrival at Hodder & Stoughton in 1965, England commissioned two works which became bestsellers: Richard Wurmbrand's *Tortured for Christ* and J.B. Phillips' *Ring of Truth*. Both these works sold well over 100,000 copies in the first year. Following the astonishing success of the *Living Bible* translation, England was made a member of the company's Board of Directors. Always on the lookout for the next classic, England felt that a major work by Packer could be a very significant publishing proposition.[2] He pointed out that the articles would have to be rewritten to make a coherent book. Packer, however, already knew this, and was willing to do what was necessary. The finishing touches to the typescript were made during a family holiday in North Wales in August 1971.

Although the book was very successful in England, it was in North America that *Knowing God* would have its greatest impact. Packer was a recognised writer in the region, having spoken at major seminaries and conferences there, but *Knowing God* would propel him to levels of fame within the evangelical community which exceeded anything he had hitherto known. James Sire was responsible for acquiring the North American rights to the book for InterVarsity Press in the United States. In May 1972, Sire travelled to Switzerland to work with Os Guinness on finalising the text of his major work *The Dust of Death* from his base at L'Abri, the community founded by Francis Schaeffer. Sire spent ten productive and enjoyable days with Guinness, completing the final edit of the text.

Sire broke his journey home in London to meet up with his editorial counterparts at InterVarsity Press and Hodder & Stoughton.

Both publishers were at that time located in Bedford Square in the centre of London, making a brief visit to both possible in a single stopover. He was introduced to Edward England, who – in the course of a short meeting lasting about fifteen minutes – showed him the text of *Knowing God*. Sire immediately asked for an option on the work, which England granted. About a week later, Hodder's page proofs arrived in the offices of InterVarsity Press in Downers Grove, Illinois. Sire showed them to Jim Nyquist, the Director of the Press and, after a few minutes spent perusing the proofs, Nyquist was convinced that they had a major work on their hands. 'Your fifteen minutes with Edward England', he told Sire, 'will be worth more to us than your ten days with Os Guinness.' *The Dust of Death* proved to be an important book, which sold very well; it was, however, eclipsed by *Knowing God*. By 1992, the work had sold more than a million copies worldwide.

So did this represent a change of direction for Packer, given his trademark emphasis on the foundational role of theology? After all, few books on theology ever make it to the bestseller lists. Yet *Knowing God* is rigorously grounded in a set of theological principles which – like the title of the book itself – can be argued to derive ultimately from the Reformer John Calvin (1509–64), for whom Packer had considerable admiration. What was new, and what gave the work its enormous appeal, was a clear and engaging demonstration of how these basic principles could be *brought* to life and *applied* to life. Given the importance of this point, it needs further consideration.

Packer on the Relation of Theology and Spirituality

The relation between theology and spirituality has become one of the most hotly debated topics in theological education since about 1980, not least because of the experience of many seminary students who found academic theology inimical to their personal faith. This whole issue was one to which Packer had given considerable thought throughout his career as a theological educator. Although he was prepared to use the term 'spirituality', he did not consider it to be quite the right one for what he understood to be at stake.

What term, then, did he prefer? In his lectures at Trinity College, Bristol, during the 1970s, Packer used the phrase 'spiritual theology' to refer to the general Christian discipline of 'conceiving and living the life of communion with God'. Although he glossed this specific activity with the term 'spirituality', Packer saw it as improper and unhelpful to treat 'spirituality' as if it were something distinct from theology. Spiritual theology concerned the proper application of systematic theology, and was not an independent discipline in its own right.

Perhaps Packer's finest and most incisive statement of his views on spiritual theology is to be found in his inaugural lecture as the first Sangwoo Yountong Chee Professor of Theology at Regent College, Vancouver. This lecture, delivered in the College chapel on 11 December 1989, and published the following year, was entitled 'An Introduction to Systematic Spirituality'. The title itself is of significance, in that it immediately suggests a close connection between 'systematic theology' and 'spirituality' – a connection which the lecture proceeded to explore and explain.[3]

Packer offered his Vancouver audience a definition of spirituality as 'enquiry into the whole Christian enterprise of pursuing, achieving, and cultivating communion with God, which includes both public worship and private devotion, and the results of these in actual Christian life'. The definition included an emphasis on the application of truth to life, which Packer had long regarded as of vital importance: 'I have always conceived theology, ethics and apologetics as truth for people, and have never felt free to leave unapplied any truth that I taught . . . To speak of the application of truth to life is to look at life as itself a relationship to God; and when one does that, one is talking about spirituality.'

For Packer, spirituality was an integral part of theological education, especially for those who were called to pastor, since 'We cannot function well as counsellors, spiritual directors and guides to birth, growth and maturity in Christ, unless we are clear as to what constitutes spiritual well-being as opposed to spiritual lassitude and exhaustion, and to stunted and deformed spiritual development.' But where do these norms come from? For Packer, the answer was clear: from systematic theology. But immediately, Packer qualified what he understood by that term, and specifically distanced himself from two inadequate yet influential understandings of the nature of that discipline. One is the liberal view that the proper subject matter of systematic theology is 'Christian feelings and ideas about God'. The other is the traditional view that systematic theology ought to be 'revealed truth about the works, ways and will of God' as disclosed in Scripture.

Packer clearly regards the first view, which he considers to be representative of F. D. E. Schleiermacher and Rudolf Bultmann, as seriously defective. Yet he also has concerns about the second view, which he associates with Protestant scholastic writers of the seventeenth century, and most of the theological writers of the evangelical theological renaissance since the Second World War – concerns which primarily relate to the way in which this approach is *applied*. We must allow Packer to express this fully in his own words:

> I question the adequacy of conceptualizing the subject-matter of systematic theology as simply revealed truths about God, and I challenge the assumption that has usually accompanied this form of statement, that the material, like other scientific data, is best studied in cool and clinical detachment. Detachment from what, you ask? Why, from the relational activity of trusting, loving, worshipping, obeying, serving and glorifying God: the activity that results from realizing that one is actually in God's presence, actually being addressed by him, every time one opens the Bible or reflects on any divine truth whatsoever. This . . . proceeds as if doctrinal study would only be muddled by introducing devotional concerns; it drives a wedge between . . . knowing true notions about God and knowing the true God himself.[4]

For Packer, 'the proper subject-matter of systematic theology is God actively relating in and through all created things to human beings'. Theology must therefore be recognised to be 'a devotional discipline, a verifying in experience of Aquinas' beautiful remark that theology is taught by God, teaches God, and takes us to God'. There is therefore a need to *bring* together, and to *hold* together, systematic theology and spirituality. 'I want to see spirituality studied within an evaluative theological frame . . . I want to arrange a marriage, with explicit exchange of vows and mutual commitments, between spirituality and theology.' That marriage can be seen at its best in Packer's *Knowing God* – to which we may now turn more fully.

Knowing God: *Some Reflections*

In this landmark work, Packer explicitly draws on some themes set out by John Calvin in his *Institutes of the Christian Religion* (1559).[5] First, a proper 'knowledge of God', in the Christian sense of the term, does not refer to some natural human awareness of God, but to a knowledge which arises within a relationship with God. Second, this knowledge of God is 'more than knowing *about* God, although knowing about God is its foundation'. Packer here draws a distinction between 'knowledge by description' and 'knowledge by acquaintance'. While it is necessary to have a correct understanding of God as the righteous, wise and merciful Creator and judge, Packer argues that a true knowledge of God must also be 'relational knowledge', by which he means a knowledge that comes to us in a 'relation of commitment and trust, faith and reliance'.

Finally, to know God is also to know God's relationship to us. Packer notes Calvin's insistence that all human wisdom consists of 'knowledge of God and of ourselves', and that these two are inseparable. To know God is to know ourselves; to know ourselves truly, we must know God. 'Knowing God' is therefore not knowing God *in isolation*; it is rather about 'knowing God in his relationship to us, that relationship in which he gives himself and his gifts to us for our enrichment'. To know God, we need to know both his gracious gifts to us, and our need for such gifts in the first place.

On the basis of this analysis, Packer concludes by declaring that 'knowing God' consists of three components, which must be taken together, and seen as inseparable aspects of a greater whole: grasping who God is; applying to ourselves what God *is* and what God *gives*; and adoring God as the one who gives these gifts. Packer's *Knowing God* can be seen as a careful exposition of these three interconnected components. His strategy is to begin by allowing his readers to apprehend the reality of God; then to move on to enable them to apply these insights to their lives; and finally, to respond to God in adoration.

It is impossible to overstress the enormous importance of this single volume in appreciating the popular appeal and influence of Packer. What, then, is so special about *Knowing God*'s particular approach? Everyone seems to find something different within its pages, a certain theme or a specific way of thinking which speaks to them with a direct relevance or power. Many have remarked to me about its pellucid prose – Packer's ability to craft forms of words that are transparent to the great truths he is exploring.[6] Whereas some use technocratic and clunky language that irritates their readers, and others highly elaborate prose that distracts readers from their core message, Packer's total immersion in his topic and his obvious command of language allow his words to become windows into the divine, functioning as a channel of grace rather than being a distraction or obstacle. My own favourite example of the effectiveness of this 'plain' style of writing is this section from Packer's discussion of 'being known' by God:

> What matters supremely, therefore, is not, in the last analysis, the fact that I know God, but the larger fact which underlies it – the fact that *he knows me*. I am graven on the palms of his hands. I am never out of his mind. All my knowledge of him depends on his sustained initiative in knowing me. I know him, because he first knew me, and continues to know me. He knows me as a friend, one who loves me; and there is no moment when his eye is off me, or his attention distracted from me, and no moment, therefore, when his care falters.[7]

The rhythms and cadences of these sentences are those of a preacher – a theologian who knows that words matter, and that those words must therefore be chosen with great care and thought, aiming to divert attention from the preacher towards the great themes of the gospel. Packer here echoes not simply the theological convictions of his Puritan forebears, but also their passion to communicate them to the hearts and minds of their audiences.

Packer often stresses his commitment to plain English – to simple, concise and clear statements. His familiarity with the great controversies over preaching in seventeenth-century England led him to prefer the Puritan 'plain' style over the 'metaphysical' or 'ornamented' styles of leading Anglican preachers, such as William Laud or Lancelot Andrewes.[8] The great Methodist preacher John Wesley frequently criticised writers and preachers who used a 'highly ornamented style', relying on oratorical techniques and lofty phrases to communicate their ideas; for Wesley, a plain style of writing and speaking enabled the preacher to focus on the message being proclaimed rather than the rhetorical techniques employed. John Henry Newman made a similar point a century later, declaring that a preacher was someone who 'has something to say and knows how to say it'.[9] Packer's *Knowing God* is not simply an outstanding work of spiritual theology; it is an affirmation of the capacity of the Puritan 'plain' style of writing to communicate profound spiritual truths without the need for verbal embellishment and adornment.

Let me pick up on some themes from *Knowing God*, and consider how Packer uses and develops them within his overall project of putting together a 'string of beads' on the great topic of knowing, and being known by, God. The first of these is found in the preface. Packer here refers to an image, devised by John Mackay, of those who theologise from a balcony, and those who theologise on the road.[10] Packer's framing device – his way of setting up a significant theological discussion – is often passed over in haste by his readers. Yet it is worth pausing here, and lingering over Packer's imagery, and the contrast he hopes to make.

John Mackay was a Reformed theologian who was serving as President of Princeton Theological Seminary when he penned his brief work *A Preface to Christian Theology* (1941), aiming to recapture the significance of Christian theology in terms of 'bringing back meaning into life' and 'restoring the foundations on which all true life and thought are built'. For Mackay, Christians use two main perspectives in trying to make sense of life and live meaningfully within the world.[11] Mackay designates one 'the Balcony' and the other 'the Road'.

So what does he mean by these terms? Mackay asks us to imagine some people sitting on the high front balcony of a Spanish town-house on a warm evening, watching the crowds walking by on the street below them. These people on the balcony – 'balconeers', as Mackay terms them – are onlookers, high above the flux of everyday life, observing things below them from a curious yet disinterested perspective. This is one way of doing theology – standing above the life of faith and failing to participate in it. For Mackay, the real busi-ness of theology is done on the road below. The Church and indi-vidual believers live out a pilgrim life on the road. The Christian is not a lone traveller, but part of a 'fellowship of the road' which seeks and hopes to find truth and meaning on the journey.

William Leathem, Packer's former colleague at St John's, Harborne, echoed Mackay's point in his contribution on the role of the local church to the National Evangelical Anglican Congress of 1967:

> To stand aloof and apart from the real world means death to the church. It will not do either to scream from the housetops or purr in the pulpit. Balcony religion is no longer acceptable, if it ever was. The Church and Christians must step down into the arena of everyday life.[12]

Packer develops this point further, stressing that those on the road 'face problems which, although they have their theoretical angle, are essentially practical – problems of the "which-way-to-go" and "how-to-make-it" type, problems which call not merely for compre-hension but for decision and action too'. As Packer makes it clear, *Knowing God* is a 'book for travellers, and it is with travellers' ques-tions that it deals'[13].

This distinction between 'balconeer' and 'traveller' is essential to grasping Packer's approach in *Knowing God*. He illustrates the impor-tance of this difference by considering the classical issue of theodicy – the question of how Christians respond to the existence of suffer-ing and evil. Is this about intellectual speculation on the origins of evil, or about coping with the realities of life, and growing in the face of suffering and evil? 'In relation to *evil*, the balconeer's problem is to find a theoretical explanation of how evil can consist with God's sovereignty and goodness, but the traveller's problem is how to master evil and bring good out of it.' Packer presents *Knowing God* as a work aimed at his fellow travellers, which draws on the wisdom of those who have journeyed this road before them. *Knowing God* deals with experiential matters – not abstract theoretical speculation but a direct engagement with the experience of knowing and been known by God.

It is not difficult to see how Packer's discussion is constantly informed by his theology; the manner of its expression and application, however, is not didactic, but rather takes the form of engaging with experience and sharing wisdom. Yet it is important to note that many Reformed theologians of the 1970s and beyond were reluctant to consider experience, seeing this as a lapse into subjectivism.[14] Packer did much to break this taboo, partly through reclaiming the richness of the Puritan heritage of experiential piety, and partly through his careful demonstration of the experiential connections, implications and consequences of Calvin's theology of the knowledge of God.

Thus Packer's account of what it means to know God is cognitive, experiential and relational. We saw earlier that the decisive issue is not 'notional correctness', which privileges academic theologians and biblical scholars. According to Packer, 'you can have all the right notions in your head, without ever tasting in your heart the realities to which they refer'.[15] Knowing God does indeed begin with knowing *about* God; but it does not stop there. To know God truly is transformative, bringing about a multilayered change within us, analogous to coming to know and love another person.

Revelation is not simply about God opening his *mind* to us; it is about God disclosing the secrets of his *heart* – a mark of privilege and intimacy: 'We must not lose sight of the fact that knowing God is an emotional relationship, as well as an intellectual and volitional one, and could not indeed be a close relationship between persons were it not so.'[16] In this way, Packer weaves together the threads of the rich biblical witness to God, bringing out the distinct identity – yet ultimate inseparability of – theology, worship, prayer, spirituality and evangelism as we travel along the road to the New Jerusalem.

Knowing God established Packer's international reputation as a constructive writer, able to bring theology and spirituality into a productive conversation, and build bridges between the Reformed and Puritan heritage and today's spiritual concerns. With such a wide constituency, stretching far beyond the Church of England or the British Isles, it was perhaps inevitable that Packer would be drawn to a new sphere of ministry beyond any specific denomination or nation, where he could speak across both denominational and national boundaries.

In the next chapter, we shall explore the developments that took Packer in a new direction and how he came to be part of the faculty of Regent College, Vancouver.

I I

The Move to Canada:
Regent College, Vancouver

The enormous success of *Knowing God* established Packer as one of the most significant evangelical theological and spiritual writers of his day. His reputation continued to grow within the evangelical constituency, particularly as a result of his Tyndale Biblical Theology Lecture delivered at Tyndale House, Cambridge, on 17 July 1973.[1] This lecture dealt with the question of what the cross achieved, and set out what many consider to be the most sophisticated defence of a substitutionary approach to understanding the death of Christ. It was, to many observers, now inevitable that Packer would be drawn to a position in North America, where he would find more time to write, speak and teach.

Packer was increasingly sought after in the United States as a figure of wisdom and maturity, particularly in the midst of the heat of some of the controversies which broke out within American evangelicalism during the 1970s, most notably over the issue of how biblical authority was to be defined and defended. Harold Lindsell's highly polemical *Battle for the Bible* (1976) advocated making commitment to biblical inerrancy a criterion of evangelical identity, even going on to suggest that the term 'evangelical' should be abandoned in favour of 'fundamentalist'.

Packer became embroiled in this vitriolic and largely unproductive debate – the only British evangelical writer to do so. His status as an outsider to the world of American evangelicalism was unquestionably an asset. Some saw the divisive dispute about biblical inerrancy as a bid for theological and institutional influence over the future direction of American evangelicalism – an attempt by the northern evangelical establishment to impose its technical language on the entire evangelical coalition in the United States. Packer had no vested interest in the controversy and was able to focus on genuinely theological issues, rather than get involved in power-bids for authority and influence dressed up as theology.

For Packer, the issue under discussion was about the 'total trustworthiness' of the Bible as a consequence of its 'entire truthfulness'. Debates about terminology – such as 'inerrancy' and 'infallibility' – can thus be seen in an informing context. Packer commented on this issue in his lectures at Regent College, Vancouver, in the fall of 1988, at a time when the debate was fizzling out: 'Inerrancy and infallibility thus become synonyms, differing only in nuance and tone (the former accenting trustworthiness as a *source*, the latter accenting trustworthiness as a *guide*). Neither word need be used; both may be used to advantage.'[2]

In part, Packer's anxiety about such overheated theological disputes was the tendency of some of their leading figures to portray opponents whose ideas they found threatening as enemies who needed to be vanquished. There were, he pointed out, real theological questions that evangelicals needed to address, and polemics got in the way of necessary theological reflection on issues such as revelation as communication, hermeneutics as a theory of understanding, the use of Scripture in preaching and theology, and how the historically relative may have absoluteness and finality for all time.[3]

Yet Packer also found himself enmeshed in controversy back in the United Kingdom, where evangelicals were increasingly under attack. James Barr's aggressively anti-evangelical *Fundamentalism* and John Hick's edited collection of essays *The Myth of God Incarnate* were both published in 1977; taken together, they constituted a formidable broadside against evangelicalism. Many British evangelicals hoped that Packer would stand up against such threats. However, paradoxically, some came to see Packer as part of the problem. Why so? The answer lies in the Church of England's Doctrine Commission.

Packer became a member of this Commission when it was chaired by the Bishop of Durham, the distinguished philosopher of religion Ian T. Ramsey. Following Ramsey's sudden death, the Chair passed to Maurice F. Wiles, who shortly afterwards published a work entitled *The Remaking of Christian Doctrine*, which reflected a strongly sceptical stance towards traditional Christian teaching. Two other academic members of the Commission were strongly critical of traditional Christian orthodoxy: Dennis Nineham declared that there was no point in trying to ground Christianity in anything that was specifically linked to the person of Jesus, while Geoffrey Lampe argued strongly against traditional views of the atonement. For Wiles, Nineham and Lampe, the central dogmas of the Christian faith required radical restatements in the light of their increasingly sceptical attitude towards them.

Packer was thus in a decided minority on the Commission, unable to influence its decisions or declarations. Its 1976 report *Christian Believing* was widely seen as anodyne, vague and lacking in the basic features of what C. S. Lewis described as 'Mere Christianity' – a generous consensual Christian orthodoxy. Some, unaware of the impossible situation in which Packer had found himself, suggested he had failed to represent biblical orthodoxy. For Packer, there was little that he could have done. He was convinced that it was right to represent evangelicalism on the Commission. Once the decision had been taken by the majority of members to use the report to describe what its members believed (rather than prescribe what ought to be believed), the outcome was inevitable. Yet it was an uncomfortable time for Packer, who began to sense he was no longer valued as a theological voice.

The Charismatic Movement

Although the origins of the charismatic movement are generally traced back to the ministry of Charles Fox Parham and events at the Azusa Street Mission, Los Angeles, in 1906–8, it was not until the 1970s that it became a major force in Western Christianity. Packer was a close observer of this development, and became an astute analyst of its significance for evangelicalism. The rediscovery of spiritual gifts is linked with the movement known as Pentecostalism, generally regarded as the first modern movement to demonstrate clearly charismatic inclinations. The full impact of the charismatic movement within evangelicalism, however, dates from the 1960s. The incident which brought it to public attention took place in Van

Nuys, California, where the Rector of the local Episcopalian church, Dennis Bennett, told his congregation that he had been filled with the Holy Spirit and had spoken in tongues. Reaction varied from bewilderment to outrage; the local Episcopalian bishop promptly banned speaking in tongues from his churches.

However, it soon became clear that others had shared Bennett's experience. Philip E. Hughes, a noted evangelical theologian and friend of Packer, witnessed the phenomenon at first hand, and wrote up his experiences for both the North American *Christianity Today* and the September 1962 edition of the British evangelical journal *The Churchman*. Hughes reported that he was convinced that 'the Breath of the Living God is stirring among the dry bones of the major, respectable, old-fashioned denominations, and particularly within the Episcopal Church'.[4] From that moment, the Holy Spirit was firmly on the agenda of British evangelicalism.

There was initially some confusion in England over what was happening though. To some, the new experiences being reported seemed capable of being explained on the basis of the Keswick holiness teaching, which interpreted them in terms of an intensification of an existing spirituality. Martyn Lloyd-Jones introduced the subject for discussion at a meeting of the Westminster Fellowship on 8 October 1962. It soon became clear that a number of younger Anglican clergy had experienced some form of charismatic renewal, with St Mark's, Gillingham, in Kent becoming an especially significant centre of renewal.

Four Anglican clergy, three of whom had served at St Mark's, Gillingham, arranged to meet Martyn Lloyd-Jones in London on 9 April 1963. At this time, Lloyd-Jones was held in high regard by many within the evangelical wing of the Church of England.[5] Lloyd-Jones listened carefully to the four describing their experiences, before telling them of something similar which had happened to him during a visit he had made to the Hebrides in the summer of 1949. Lloyd-Jones concluded that they had 'been baptised in the Holy Spirit'.

There is little doubt that the charismatic movement has brought fresh life to the Church through its rediscovery of the role of the Holy Spirit in Christian life and experience. Yet this new emphasis

upon the role of the Holy Spirit brought with it tensions and controversy, most notably over the issue of the importance of experience of
the Spirit in the normal Christian life, and the relation between
Word and Spirit. Packer has been a significant theological voice –
indeed, at times, it has to be said, a lonely voice – in this important
discussion since the late 1960s.[6] We have already noted Packer's strategy, evident in his involvement in the book *Growing into Union*, of
collaborating wherever possible with others who were committed to
basic Christian orthodoxy, despite differences that might exist
between them over matters of church order (see p. 93). By the early
1970s, it was clear to Packer that the charismatic movement was
coming of age and needed to be taken seriously and viewed positively by evangelicals.

The growing strength of the charismatic movement gave new
relevance to Packer's desire and ability to bridge the theological and
experiential divide between classic evangelicalism and the movement
itself. Packer's concern for spirituality and evangelical collaboration
led to him taking this new movement seriously, where other senior
evangelical figures tended to dismiss it as a theological fad. Packer
was one of the few actively working during the 1970s in England to
forge bridges in this way, at a time when many senior evangelicals
within the Church of England were inclined to view the movement
with hostility, especially over the issue of 'baptism in the Spirit'.

The Senior Eclectic Conference of 1974 brought together a
number of leading evangelicals, including John Stott, to discuss the
progress made since the National Evangelical Anglican Congress of
1967 (see p. 77). Packer was present, and offered a survey of developments since Keele, highlighting issues which arose from the growing
strength of the charismatic movement. Surely, Packer argued, the
time had come for non-charismatic evangelicals to appreciate that
there was sufficient 'essential evangelicalism' within the charismatic
movement to allow the former to begin to relate to the latter in
strongly positive terms; it seemed only right to start working with
them on matters of importance.[7]

On the basis of Packer's address, John Stott decided the time was
indeed right to start exploring ways of strengthening links between
evangelicals and charismatics, and invited Packer and John Baker (a

noted Calvinist who trained at Tyndale Hall, Bristol) to draft a discussion document. The 'Gospel and Spirit' group (as it came to be known) drew together leading evangelicals from the Church of England Evangelical Council (including both Stott and Packer) and charismatics (including Michael Harper and David Watson). The group met together for four day-conferences over a period of eighteen months and was finally able to issue a joint statement. It is widely agreed that this statement was of fundamental importance in ensuring that the charismatic issue would not be a cause of division at the Second National Evangelical Anglican Congress of 1977 – to which we now turn.

Nottingham: The Second National Evangelical Anglican Congress

In 1974, John Stott and other evangelical leaders felt it was time to take steps to consolidate the work and extend the influence of the National Evangelical Anglican Congress, held at Keele in 1967.[8] The Church of England Evangelical Council, the Church Society and the Church Pastoral Aid Society agreed to plan a second Congress to mark a decade since Keele, which was now recognised as marking a decisive change in the mood of evangelicalism within the Church of England. The backdrop to this development was a growing sense that Keele had not delivered what some had hoped for: greater evangelical influence within the national Church of England. Its greatest tactical success – the defeat of the scheme for Anglican and Methodist unity – had been defeated only through an alliance with Anglo-Catholics, whose reasons for opposing the scheme were radically different from those proposed by evangelicals, such as Packer.

Whereas the Keele Congress of 1967 was given strategic direction by a small group with close links to Latimer House, led by Stott and Packer, a much larger planning committee was brought together for its 1977 successor. Packer felt that the proposed Congress would be a distraction, which would get in the way of carrying forward the vision of the Keele Congress in local churches. Packer was in a minority at this point; most took the view that a second Congress was needed. At the second planning meeting, disagreements again emerged. Packer took the view that the proposed Congress ought to focus on a specific theme of importance, such as ethics. Stott, however, felt that a conference could only have significant appeal if it addressed as wide a range of issues as was reasonably possible. In the end, his view prevailed. Finally, Packer suggested there was little point in the Congress producing a report, given the wide range of issues it intended to consider. Once more, Packer was in a minority. An Executive Committee, chaired by John Scott, was created to organise the Congress, which would be held at the Sports Hall of the University of Nottingham in the East Midlands over the period Thursday, 14 April to Monday, 18 April 1977. It is significant that Packer was not a member of this committee;[9] from the outset, he appeared to be peripheral to the event.

The Nottingham Congress was well attended, attracting twice the number that came to Keele. Discussion focused on the contents of three volumes that served as study guides for the event: 'The Lord Christ', 'The Changing World' and 'The People of God'. Packer contributed a carefully worded defence and application of the 'Lordship of Christ'.[10] It was a solid, intelligent and persuasive theological reflection, which ranks as one of his most constructive pieces. Yet it received little attention, particularly in comparison with Anthony Thiselton's paper on hermeneutics, which highlighted the danger of attempting to force the Bible to answer distinctively modern questions to which the text itself does not specifically refer. Thiselton's paper set the scene for the Conference's final statement, which referenced Thiselton's ideas – though not naming him explicitly – in many of its pronouncements concerning contemporary biblical interpretation and application.

The Nottingham Congress was useful in allowing Anglican evangelicals to reflect on a series of notable theological and practical issues, even if it can now be seen to have failed to offer a persuasive rationale for being both Anglican and evangelical, other than for reasons for convenience and opportunity. Packer himself realised that there was an 'Anglican evangelical identity problem', and published an important and oft-cited pamphlet on this question once the dust of the Congress had settled.[11] His misgivings had, however, been heightened by some younger voices at the Nottingham Congress, who seemed to reject or downplay the significance of matters which he considered to be critically important. David Watson, then noted for his influential evangelistic ministry in the city of York and in the student world, declared that 'the Reformation was one of the greatest tragedies that ever happened to the church'.[12] The Congress made no reference in any of its statements to the ongoing role of the Thirty-Nine Articles which were, for Packer and others, a means of affirming the historical commitment of the Church of England to theological orthodoxy.

Packer was also alarmed that one of the core identity-markers of conservative evangelicalism seemed to have been sidelined by the Congress. Historically, evangelicalism had once regarded the doctrine of penal substitution as the only valid means of interpreting the cross of Christ. However, the doctrine came under mounting criticism during the later nineteenth century, and subsequently during the twentieth. Packer had responded to those concerns in his 1973 Tyndale lecture (see p. 113), reaffirming the substitutionary nature of Christ's death. Yet the Nottingham Congress made it clear that there was increasing reluctance on the part of many evangelicals to commit themselves exclusively to this traditional evangelical understanding of the atonement – a concern clearly formulated in its Final Statement:

> Regarding the Atonement, we all gladly affirm that the death and resurrection of Jesus is the heart of the gospel of salvation: 'Christ died for our sins in accordance with the Scriptures, and was raised on the third day'. Nevertheless, we give different emphasis to the various biblical expressions of the Atonement. Some see the truth that Christ died in our place as the central explanation of the cross, while others, who also give this truth a position of great importance, lay greater stress on the relative significance of the other biblical pictures.[13]

Given the future course of his career, it would be easy to suggest that Packer felt that he did not really belong in the new world of evangelical Anglicanism, and that this caused him to leave England and settle somewhere else where he believed he had an ongoing role to play. Perhaps, however, it might be more accurate to suggest that Packer's growing sense of disconnection with the changing mood and agendas of evangelicalism within the Church of England made him more receptive to offers of alternative ministries. Whatever Packer chose, it would not be more of the same. He needed a new platform for his ministry – and the most obvious location for such a ministry was in an American seminary with roots in the Reformed tradition, such as Westminster Theological Seminary, Philadelphia, or a distinctively evangelical seminary, such as Trinity Evangelical Divinity School, located just north of Chicago. In the end, however, the call which changed the course of his life came from western Canada.

Regent College, Vancouver

The origins of Regent College, Vancouver – now firmly established as a premier evangelical graduate school of theology – go back to the late 1960s, when a series of prominent evangelicals, many with links to the Christian Brethren, recognised the need for a new school of theology with a focus on the laity.[14] A number of factors led to the emergence of this vision. Many admired Francis Schaeffer's L'Abri community as a Christian study centre yet felt it would have greater impact if it were located within a major university, while maintaining its evangelical identity.[15] Regent College was founded in 1968 as the first graduate school of theology in North America to make education of the laity its central focus. Its first educational venture was a summer school in 1969, which drew fifty-six students to St Andrew's Hall on the University of British Columbia campus.

In 1970, Regent College appointed James Houston as its first Principal, and set up its offices and teaching space in the basement of Union Theological College, a Presbyterian school of ministry on the University site. Houston was quite clear what sort of institution he hoped to create. First, unlike Schaeffer's L'Abri, it would be located on a campus and have some formal affiliation with that university. Second, the new college should be a graduate school of theology,

rather than a 'Bible school'. And third, it would be transdenominational and evangelical in its outlook. It was a vision that clearly
appealed to many. The College's reputation and enrolment quickly
grew and in 1972 it began offering what proved to be its trademark
qualification: the Master of Christian Studies.

Houston's second and third goals were arguably fulfilled by 1972.
In 1974, Houston finally achieved the first of his three goals through
securing both the College's affiliation with the University of British
Columbia and moving the College to new premises on Vancouver's
Wesbrook Mall, taking over two former university fraternity houses
for its administration and teaching. Houston was now in a position
to begin to expand his faculty. The three core faculty staff in the
College's first years were Ward Gasque, Assistant Professor of New
Testament; Carl E. Armerding, Assistant Professor of Old Testament;
and Houston himself, who taught in the area of 'interdisciplinary
and environmental studies'. Houston knew he needed to attract a
theologian who was capable of relating to lay students, and who
could teach across denominational boundaries.

In 1974, Houston appointed Clark H. Pinnock as Regent
College's first Associate Professor of Systematic and Christian
Theology. It was an excellent choice. Pinnock was a Canadian, who
had studied under F. F. Bruce at Manchester and subsequently served
as Professor of New Testament and Systematic Theology at New
Orleans Baptist Theological Seminary. He thus had the international
experience which Houston wished to foster within Regent College.
Pinnock had established himself as a leading younger theologian
within North American evangelicalism through major writings on
the areas of revelation and apologetics, including *A Defense of Biblical
Infallibility* (1967), *Set Forth Your Case* (1967), *Evangelism and Truth*
(1969) and *Biblical Revelation: The Foundation of Christian Theology*
(1971). Pinnock's growing reputation attracted more students to the
College. But in 1977, Pinnock moved east to take up a position at
McMaster Divinity School, Ontario.

So who could Houston find to replace Pinnock? A huge gap
loomed, not simply in Regent's teaching faculty, but also in its international reputation and potential ability to attract students. There
was an urgent need to find a major international theologian, whose

personal stature would ensure Regent's continued reputational excellence in this area. Houston's mind wandered back to the 1940s, when Packer – then a young Oxford undergraduate – attended his local Brethren church in east Oxford. He had made quite a name for himself since those early days. But would he be interested in coming to Canada? There was only one way to find out. At just after three o'clock in the morning local time, Houston lifted his phone and placed an international call.

Packer remembers what happened well. He was working in his study at Trinity College, Bristol, one morning in 1976, when the telephone rang at 11.10 a.m. The caller turned out to be Houston, who asked Packer whether he would be interested in a Chair of Theology at Regent College which Clark Pinnock was in the process of vacating. Packer knew about Regent; he had visited the institution, and thoroughly concurred with what he found, especially its implicit emphasis on breaking down the barriers between clergy and laity. He asked Houston to write his ideas down, and he would give the possibility careful thought. This was not the first invitation Packer had received to relocate to the other side of the Atlantic, and he had become quite used to turning such approaches down with a diplomatic, gentle firmness. He expected to decline this invitation equally graciously.

Houston's letter arrived a week later. As Packer read it, he began to realise that the proposal was, in fact, a serious possibility. For reasons we have explored, he was frustrated with his situation in England, and could see no hope of things improving in the next few years. He knew and respected Houston from their time together in Oxford in the late 1940s, and the prospect of working alongside him was attractive. Houston was committed to the idea of peer-parity within the faculty of Regent College, a model which Packer had tried to ensure was incorporated into the structure of Trinity College at the time of the merger.

Taking up a professorship at Regent College would also fit in well with his bilateral strategy, which led him to concentrate on both Anglicanism and transdenominational evangelicalism. This strategy would have been difficult to implement if he held a position at a denominational seminary in the United States – such as Westminster

Theological Seminary. In England, he was employed at an Anglican theological school, and was able to make this his base for a transdenominational ministry; if he went to Regent, he would be employed at a transdenominational school, which he could use as a base for his ministry within Anglicanism.

Furthermore, Packer liked Vancouver in particular, and Canada in general, which seemed to him to be culturally half-way between Britain and the United States. If he had to move to somewhere in North America, his preference would be for Canada rather than the United States. Packer's mother had died in 1965, and his father in 1972. He thus had no further family responsibilities in England. His children's education could be arranged. Yet perhaps the decisive factor was that moving to Regent College would allow him more time to write. It was an important consideration, for Packer was clear that an integral part of his vocation was to write the books which would encourage, sustain and inform the Church.

After much thought, Packer wrote to Houston, telling him he was minded to accept his offer, but would not be in a position to move before 1979. Packer felt he needed to wait sufficiently long after the Nottingham Congress of 1977 before announcing his move, as he did not wish his decision to leave England to be interpreted as an implied criticism of what had happened at the Congress.

Encouraged by this positive (though not definitive) response, Houston began the faculty recruitment procedure at Regent. During one of his tours of North America, Packer inconspicuously spent a period of twenty-four hours at Regent. He later discovered that Klaus Bockmuehl (then teaching at St Chrischona Theological Seminary in Switzerland) was also being interviewed for a faculty position at the College, Houston having approached him in much the same way as he had Packer. Initially, the College's financial situation led the Regent College Council to conclude they would have to choose between Packer and Bockmuehl; by the end of their discussions, however, the decision had swung to employing them both.

Packer's inclination to accept the offer was clinched by a tipping factor – the appointment of Harry S. D. Robinson, a noted evangelical known to Packer, to become Rector of St John's Church, Shaughnessy, not far from Regent College. One of the reasons why

Packer was hesitant about a move to Vancouver was the apparent absence of a suitable Anglican parish in which he could minister. When Robinson offered Packer an honorary assistantship in his parish, it seemed that all the pieces of a vocational puzzle had fallen into place. However, Packer wanted to be sure that Kit would approve of this radical move.

Packer came to his final decision to accept the position during the Regent College summer school of 1978. He and Kit had been invited to spend three weeks in Vancouver, enabling Packer to teach a basic course in systematic theology. Packer was clear that he could not make a final commitment without allowing Kit to experience Vancouver at first hand and decide whether she felt she could settle there. This period of immersion proved to be the final stage in the process of acceptance. On learning that Kit believed she could live happily in Vancouver, Packer agreed to accept firmly the offer which had been made to him. The announcement was then made, at the end of Packer's contribution to the summer school, that he would return in September 1979 to take up a full-time faculty position at Regent College.

A new phase – perhaps a golden phase – had opened in Packer's life. The announcement was greeted with delight in Vancouver, and with surprise and sadness back in England. Yet with the benefit of hindsight, it was not merely a good move; it was the right move. Packer flourished at Regent College, consolidating his reputation as a classic conservative evangelical theologian with a passionate concern for relating his theology to spirituality, ministry and the Bible.

Since Packer was so often described as a 'conservative' thinker, we must once more interrupt our narrative, and consider what this might mean.

12

Conservatism: Holding on to What is Good

Packer was a conservative Christian thinker. Yet though this observation is easily stated, it needs careful and attentive unpacking. The idea of being 'conservative' has come to have cultural and political associations which are not helpful in understanding what it means to describe Packer in this way. It is certainly true that Packer identified himself as both a 'conservative Christian' and a 'conservative evangelical'. He also had certain views – on the role of the family or the ministry of women, for instance – that would mark him off as a conservative thinker. But Packer saw his commitment to such views as resting on his reading of the Bible, rather than on a conservative ideology.

The best starting point in gaining an understanding here is the biblical text which underlies so much of his thinking on this question: 'test everything; hold fast what is good' (1 Thessalonians 5:21). This text does not speak of an uncritical affirmation and acceptance of everything, but of a critical process of sifting and refining, aimed at capturing and then preserving what is 'good' and that which really matters. The British philosopher Roger Scruton was one of the most able and reflective conservative philosophers of our age. In his influential book *Conservatism*, Scruton puts his finger on two themes that lie at the heart of a conservative way of thinking: 'the conviction that good things are more easily destroyed than created, and the determination to hold on to those good things in the face of politically engineered change'.[1] The same conviction and determination are evident in Packer's writings.

For Packer, this is often expressed in terms of inhabiting, exploring and expressing the 'Great Tradition'. The word 'tradition' comes from the Latin term *traditio* which encompasses such significant notions as 'handing over', 'handing down' or 'handing on'. Understood in this sense, it is a thoroughly biblical idea. Paul reminded his readers that he was handing on to them core teachings of the Christian faith which he had received from others (1 Corinthians 15:1–4). The term 'tradition' conveys two related senses, as it can refer to both the action of passing teachings on to others – something which Paul insists must be done within the Church – and to teachings themselves which are passed on in this manner. Tradition can thus be understood as a process as well as a body of teaching. The Pastoral Epistles in particular stress the importance of 'guard[ing] the good deposit entrusted to you' (2 Timothy 1:14).

Yet there is an issue here that needs further reflection, which was neatly expressed by Jaroslav Pelikan during his period as an historical theologian at Yale University: 'Tradition is the living faith of the dead, traditionalism is the dead faith of the living. And, I suppose I should add, it is traditionalism that gives tradition such a bad name.'[2] Pelikan's point is that we can only too easily allow ourselves to become enslaved by the past, feeling we have to repeat and affirm everything said or practised by earlier generations as a mark of fidelity to our tradition, or as an affirmation of the trustworthiness of a traditional interpretation of the Bible. Theologians and church leaders in the past have made mistakes. Sometimes they developed habits of thought and practice that worked well in their cultural contexts, but no longer work in our very different present-day situations. To give an obvious example: Calvin's ministry in Geneva in the 1540s and 1550s was at many points genuinely innovative and creative; but why retain his particular structures and practices today, given that many scholars believe they were developed with the specific Genevan context of the 1540s and 1550s in mind?

We need to find a way of being able to approach the legacy of the past critically yet constructively, filtering out what we might now consider to be mistaken or irrelevant, and holding on to what is good, right and useful. If we get this wrong, we find ourselves needlessly and pointlessly locked into the past; if we get it right, we are able to draw on the treasures of the legacy of the theological past, such as its reading of Scripture, allowing it to enrich our ministries and thinking today.

Let's return to Packer's period as a curate at St John's Church, Harborne, in the early 1950s. At that time, St John's stood firmly within a conservative evangelical tradition. This was obvious in several ways, such as William Leathem's commitment to expository preaching, and his concern for evangelism. The church's alignment with a classic Protestant outlook was also signalled *visually*: St John's was what was then known as a 'Black Gown' church, in that its clergy followed the pattern set by John Calvin and other sixteenth-century Genevan reformers in wearing dark gowns, rather than clerical robes, when preaching.

In the twenty-first century, few if any evangelicals in the Church of England wear black gowns, regarding it as a tradition that no longer serves any useful purpose. It may have been important once, but by the 1960s it was coming to be seen as a liability – a visual signal of being locked in the past and unwilling to adapt to a rapidly changing cultural context. Yet a commitment to expository preaching and a concern for evangelism remained integral to evangelicalism during this period of transition. We therefore need to decide what aspects of the past are essential, and which are optional, and ask when does a traditional practice become a liability, having once been an asset?

Packer sets out his own approach in his 1992 essay 'The Comfort of Conservatism', a highly accessible account of the potential role that tradition might play in the stabilisation of evangelicalism.[3] As he rightly notes, the term 'conservatism' has two 'tones' or meanings: a 'heroic resolve to preserve whatever in one's heritage one sees to be truly valuable'; and a stubborn 'adherence to what is old and conventional just because it is old and conventional'.[4] Packer's vision of conservatism parallels Scruton's. It demands a 'responsible use of one's intelligence and critical judgement, and also to swim against the cultural tide when necessary'.

For Packer, conservatism is not traditionalism – a 'backward-looking fixity' – a misguided though understandable attempt to retreat to the safety of the past, but to live meaningfully and authentically in the present through being rooted and anchored in a living tradition. It involves a process of sifting and reflection, respecting but not revering the past, aiming to identify and affirm what needs to be valued, treasured and preserved. The Christian past consists of an extended engagement with the Bible, which can be *helpful* to us as we consider our interpretative options, but which cannot be seen as *normative* for us. Every reading of Scripture, past and present, needs to be judged against the biblical text itself: 'We can gather from the early Fathers to the present an invaluable resource for understanding the Bible responsibly. Nevertheless, those interpretations (traditions) are never final; they need always to be submitted to Scripture for further review.'[5]

Like Pelikan, Packer is aware of the danger of traditionalism – the 'absolutizing of formulations and fashions that are human, not divine, and, because human, provisional and open to change'.[6] Such a 'culture-defying traditionalism' is easily represented as Christian faithfulness, when it is little more than a refusal to engage with the phenomenon of cultural change. It leads to a 'magic-word mentality', which identifies Christian orthodoxy with using the right theological terms or formulae (Packer has in mind here debates about biblical inerrancy, which often concentrated on the word 'inerrancy', rather than its intended meaning).

Having rejected this unworkable traditionalism, Packer sets out an approach by which he believes that what is wise, good and true from the past can be discerned, and gladly and joyfully reappropriated by today's Church: 'Tradition allows us to stand on the shoulders of the many giants who have thought about Scripture before us.'[7] Rediscovering the historic and corporate dimensions of our faith makes the great treasures and resources of the Christian past accessible and available to the present, thus enriching the life and witness of modern evangelicalism. We are enabled, as Packer puts it, to 'receive nurturing truth and wisdom from God's faithfulness in past generations'.

In commending the recovery of tradition as an antidote to individualism or an excessive reliance on the theological or cultural norms of the present, Packer is aware that he might be open to misunderstanding. A concern for tradition is not, he stresses, equivalent to 'traditionalism'; that is to say, a nostalgic and backward-looking approach to the Christian faith which 'can quench the Holy Spirit and cause paralysis and impotence in the church' by demanding that we blindly repeat exactly what evangelicals did and said back in the 1950s, the 1920s, the 1820s or the 1730s (or whatever period in evangelical history happens to be regarded as a 'golden age' by its advocates).

Packer is quite clear that a concern for tradition does not violate the evangelical emphasis upon the sole and supreme authority of Scripture. Tradition serves the Church in a *ministerial* mode and does not exercise authority *magisterially*. Packer's position is characteristic of the mainline Reformation of the sixteenth century, represented by both Luther and Calvin.[8] It differs, however, from the movement known as the 'Radical Reformation' or 'Anabaptism', which was strongly critical of allowing any role to tradition. For Packer, tradition is there to help and to guide, but not to command. 'Scripture must have the last word on all human attempts to state its meaning, and tradition, viewed as a series of such human attempts, has a ministerial rather than a magisterial role.' In the end, all interpretations of Scripture must be judged in the light of Scripture itself, acknowledging that the Church – including evangelicals – has misunderstood the Bible in the past.

> We are all beneficiaries of good, wise, and sound tradition, and victims of poor, unwise, and unsound traditions. This is where the absolute 'last word' of Scripture must sort out the wheat from the chaff. Hence the apostle Paul's counsel: 'Test everything. Hold on to the good' (1 Thessalonians 5:21).

As Packer pointed out in his earliest major writing, *'Fundamentalism' and the Word of God* (1958), the Christian past provides a resource for the evangelical present. As we seek to interpret Scripture and unfold its many treasures, we can learn from the wisdom of the past.

> The Spirit has been active in the Church from the first, doing the work he was sent to do – guiding God's people into an understanding of revealed truth. The history of the Church's labour to understand the Bible forms a commentary on the Bible which we cannot despise or ignore without dishonouring the Holy Spirit. To treat the principle of biblical authority as a prohibition against

reading and learning from the book of church history is not an evangelical, but an Anabaptist mistake.[9]

Tradition, for Packer, is thus something that must be judged, not received uncritically. It can all too easily shape our readings of Scripture, highlighting some ideas and obscuring others. All Protestants, Packer suggests, stand within traditions, whether Anglican or Baptist, Pentecostal or Dispensationalist, Reformed or Lutheran, Methodist or Mennonite, which open our eyes to some things and close them to others: 'All traditions function as blinders, focusing our vision on some things at which we have been taught to look constantly and that we therefore see clearly, but keeping us from seeing other things that other traditions grasp better.'[10] As a consequence, Christians of different traditions ought to talk to each other, helping each other identify and rectify blind spots, and ensuring that the totality of Scripture is illuminated and applied to life and thought.

As a historian, Packer is aware how tradition predisposes us to read the Bible in certain ways, without realising how that seemingly 'obvious' or 'self-evident' interpretation of the Bible actually gains its power or plausibility from tradition. A time-honoured way of reading the Bible is not necessarily right! Perhaps just as importantly, Packer points out how past controversies cast their long, lingering shadows over contemporary readings of the Bible: 'Many Protestants have so reacted against Roman Catholic sacramentalism as to mistrust the sacraments entirely and in practice to deny their importance.'

Packer suggests that there are three ways in which engaging positively and critically with tradition opens the way to proper biblical interpretation and theological reflection.[11]

1. *By liberating us from our own thoughts.* We need to be challenged by alternative perspectives: 'We need the discipline of learning with the saints, past and present, in the ways noted above, to counterbalance our lopsidedness and to help us break out of the narrow circle of our own present thoughts into a larger vision and a riper wisdom.'

2. *By helping us avoid being locked into today's ways of thinking.* Packer argues that attentiveness to the past liberates us from

'chronological snobbery', and alerts us to the richness of past readings of Scripture. 'Keeping regular company with yesterday's great
teachers' opens our eyes to wisdom that is otherwise denied to us.

3. *By setting us free from the limitations of our own traditions.*
Developing his earlier argument, Packer stresses that 'the tradition that shaped us had a narrowing as well as an enriching
effect on us'. Illustrating this from his own Anglican heritage,
he urges his readers to value what is good, yet identify what is
weak – and that means listening to other perspectives, past and
present.

Packer's intimate knowledge and experience of North American
evangelicalism led him to appreciate the dangers of individualism,
which seemed to him to engender a dangerously superficial and
ephemeral form of Christianity. For Packer, tradition is an antidote
against precisely such an individualism. North American evangelicalism, steeped in individualism, often seems to have no real sense of
historical 'belonging' or rootedness. As such, it is radically prone to
destabilisation.

Too often, as Packer comments, the North American evangelical
has been 'a spiritual lone ranger who has proudly or impatiently
turned his back on the church and his heritage'. Rediscovering the
corporate and historic nature of the Christian faith reduces the
danger of entire communities of faith being misled by charismatic
individuals, and affirms the ongoing importance of the Christian past
as a stabilising influence in potentially turbulent times.

Packer's approach to conservatism invites evangelicals to rediscover
their connection with historic Christianity. It is an important strategy,
which resonates particularly with some problems within American
evangelicalism – most notably, its historical rootlessness. This concern
prompted many evangelicals in North America to convert to
Catholicism or Orthodoxy (such as Peter Gillquist, the former leader
of the evangelical organisation Campus Crusade, and Frank Schaeffer,
son of the noted Calvinist apologist Francis Schaeffer).

This approach has much to offer the Christian churches, especially evangelicalism. It encourages a process of respectful yet critical dialogue with the past, determined as a matter of principle to

learn from its wisdom, while being liberated from mechanical and wooden repetitions of its judgements. Its vision of theology is corporate, rather than individualist, while creating space for individuals to make a difference to how the community perceives and articulates its foundational beliefs. It is rigorously grounded in Scripture on the one hand, while taking into account the long history of faithful Christian engagement with the Bible on the other. Packer's critical distinction between 'magisterial' and 'ministerial' approaches to tradition enables us to see writers like Luther, Calvin and Jonathan Edwards as helpful in informing and nourishing our faith, *without displacing or undermining the place of the Bible itself.* The Bible retains its authority, which is served and illuminated by its wise interpreters.

Packer's approach allows some of the anxieties within the evangelical community over the concept of tradition to be addressed and resolved. In particular, he deals with two issues that are known to be a difficulty to some. The first is that tradition can be seen as a human invention or fabrication, in opposition to the Word of God. The New Testament certainly notes this type of tradition and is vigorously critical of both the notion itself and its consequences. Packer's critical approach allows such inappropriate traditions to be identified and sifted out. OK

Second, tradition carries with it the sense of 'traditionalist' – the dead hand of previous generations, which demands that we continue to think and act in precisely the same manner as earlier generations, thus locking evangelicalism into a sixteenth-, eighteenth- or nineteenth-century worldview. To give authority of any kind to 'tradition' might therefore seem to run the risk of condemning evangelicalism to sleep-walking with the dead. In an age that is acutely aware of the importance of public perceptions of Christianity – witness the growth of 'seeker-sensitive' worship services – a concern for tradition seems totally out of place. Packer, however, argues that to value tradition, as he understands the notion, is about being rooted in and connected with the past, thus allowing the Church to be resourced by, yet not imprisoned within, its past. Like C. S. Lewis before him, Packer affirms that there is something about classic orthodoxy that gives it an appeal across time and culture.[12] YES

Questions, of course, remain, on the application of the process of critical reflection that Packer identifies as underlying the responsible use of tradition in the life of the Church. His own view on a range of questions relating to ministerial practice and sexual ethics would be described as 'conservative'. Packer's 2002 decision to leave the Anglican Church of Canada over the change in policy of the Diocese of New Westminster on blessing same-sex unions reflects his conviction that the biblical warrant for the traditional position is so secure that it would have been impossible for him to remain within a denomination that treated the Bible in such a dismissive manner.[13] Some suggested that this was essentially a 'difference about interpretation'; Packer himself saw it as going beyond the 'legitimation of sin', basing this judgement on his reading of the New Testament as a whole, particularly its views on creation, sin, regeneration and sanctification.

Yet although Packer himself did not believe in the ordination of women to ordained ministry, he did not see the commitment of either the Church of England or the Anglican Church of Canada to this practice as requiring that he separate himself from them. In 1991, *Christianity Today* carried an article by Packer titled 'Let's Stop Making Women Presbyters'.[14] Packer suggested that the fundamental reason why so many mainline denominations – including his own – were ordaining women as presbyters 'owes more to secular, pragmatic, and social factors than to any regard for biblical authority'. The New Testament, Packer argued, envisaged a 'presbyterate of manly men'. Why not remain true to this vision, rather than turning women into 'substitute men'?

This essay, it may be noted, was not well received at Regent College, Vancouver, which had a relatively high number of women students. Gordon Fee, who served as Regent's Professor of New Testament at this time, played a prominent role in Christians for Biblical Equality, and later authored a work entitled *Discovering Biblical Equality: Complementarity without Hierarchy* (2004). Packer's critics pointed out that, in the first place, he was constructing a 'universal church order' on the basis of a few biblical verses, when other sections of the New Testament pointed in a different direction; and in the second, was inconsistent in the implementation of his own principles

by allowing women to minister under male supervision.[15] To his critics, Packer here seemed to be an ecclesial traditionalist.

But it is perhaps unfair to judge the value of Packer's commenda-
tion of tradition because of potential difficulties in its application to
such complex and contested issues. Roger Scruton makes similar
points in his analysis of the potential of conservatism, highlighting
the value of Russell Kirk's *Conservative Mind* (1953) in setting out an
intellectually vigorous and defensible vision of conservatism,[16]
grounded in a firm belief in a transcendent order which was equally
capable of inspiring the poetry of T. S. Eliot and undergirding political and social attitudes.[17]

Perhaps, as Scruton suggests, conservatism is best seen as both a
conviction and a process: a determination to hold on to what is
good, lest it be lost; and a process of sifting which helps us identify
what really matters, so that it can be preserved and applied to the
needs of our day. If so, Packer offers us a luminous example of a
reflective religious conservatism capable of development and expansion in the future. As Scruton points out, such a conservatism is too
easily ridiculed as a nostalgia for an 'old and misremembered way of
life' or a 'failure of compassion' towards new ways of living. Yet as
Packer himself makes clear, when rightly understood, it provides a
basis for life and thought which affirms and values what really
matters. When all is said and done, however, what some may consider
to be an insuperable difficulty remains – namely, how a good and
valued principle formulated in one cultural context finds its proper
implementation in historically distant cultural contexts.

Perhaps the abiding importance of Packer's approach, though, is
to sensitise us to the value of the past and to alert us to the need to
value its ideas as much as those of the present. It is helpful to consider
the wise remarks of Henry Mintzberg of the Canadian Centre for
Management Development in this respect:

> There is a terrible bias in today's management literature toward
> the current, the latest, the 'hottest.' This does a disservice, not
> only to all those wonderful old writers, but especially to the read-
> ers who are all too frequently offered the trivial new instead of the
> significant old.[18]

As we have seen, Packer's approach highlights the constant value of seeking for the 'significant old' in matters of spirituality and theology, and being wary of the untested 'trivial new'.

In the previous chapter, we considered how Packer came to join the faculty of Regent College, Vancouver. Now we shall return to that narrative to see how he developed this platform for his programme of theological reflection.

13

The Golden Years: Ministry in Vancouver

Packer began his teaching at Regent College, Vancouver, in September 1979. By then, the reputation of the school was soaring; 140 students had registered for that academic year. Yet Regent College was in the process of change. James Houston was no longer the Principal, having been replaced by Carl Amerding, who brought in a series of measures designed to enhance the appeal and profile of the College, most notably setting up an MDiv course.

In the mid-1970s, Regent was a tiny institution, using borrowed rooms; by the end of the 1980s, the College was the largest graduate institution of theological education in the region, with a new purpose-built home on a premier site on the University campus. There is no doubt that Packer played a major role in ensuring the continuing rise in fame of the school; his presence at Regent College considerably increased its reputation in North America and beyond, and acted as a powerful draw for student recruitment. The year 1985 was a landmark for Regent, in that it secured accreditation from the Association of Theological Schools in the face of intense opposition from other Canadian schools (including Vancouver School of Theology) who clearly regarded Regent as a major competitor.

As numbers burgeoned, the old buildings came increasingly under strain. In 1985, the year in which accreditation was achieved, the College was attracting nearly 450 students. Two converted fraternity houses were simply not able to cope with these large numbers and it was clear that new premises were required. After careful negotiations with the University of British Columbia, a suitable building site (consisting of the old fraternity house site and the adjacent vacant corner lot at the intersection of Wesbrook Mall and University Boulevard) was secured and funds raised. The completed building was opened in 1989, a tangible symbol of the new strength of the College and the ethos which it represented. The imposing building, fronted by a small park and occupying a prime site on the eastern perimeter of the University campus, physically expresses the College's embeddedness within the wider University community.

The distinctiveness of Regent College has been framed in different ways over its history, as its self-understanding has crystallised. Its original qualification was the Master of Christian Studies. Many senior academics track their origins back to this qualification – such as Janet Martyn Soskice, Professor of Philosophical Theology at the University of Cambridge, and Nigel Biggar, Regius Professor of Moral and Pastoral Theology at the University of Oxford. The school portrayed itself as a school of theology for the laity, helping its students to integrate their faith with real life. Although the College gained the right to offer an MDiv – the core qualification for seminarians – from 1980, most Regent graduates actually went on to become lawyers, doctors, business leaders or authors.

Although Packer's primary focus in England had been on the education of future clergy, he adapted easily – and, it must be said, enthusiastically – to the education of intelligent and reflective lay people, who wanted to develop a coherent and satisfying Christian framework and apply this to their lives. Packer's approach in *Knowing God* proved meaningful and helpful to such students. Throughout his time at Regent College, Packer's primary teaching commitment was in historical and systematic theology. He offered four main lecture courses, each directly based on teaching which he had carefully developed and perfected during his time at Trinity College, Bristol:

- Systematic Theology I: Knowledge of God;
- Systematic Theology II: Doctrine of God, Creation and Man;
- Systematic Theology III: Christology and Soteriology;
- Systematic Theology IV: Ecclesiology and Eschatology.

Packer also offered additional courses, particularly for the Regent College summer schools. In addition to this demanding teaching programme, Packer and Kit were involved in the pastoral care of students. A College 'Community Group' would meet weekly at their home at 2398 West 34th Street, while Kit was also active in the College wives' group.

Packer's initial appointment at Regent College was as Professor of Historical and Systematic Theology. However, his reputational capital was such that ten years later, on 11 December 1989, Packer was formally installed as the first Sangwoo Youtong Chee Professor of Theology. This chair (which was almost invariably referred to as the 'Chee Chair' in internal Regent discussions) had been endowed by two prominent members of Vancouver's increasingly significant Chinese community in memory of their father. It was Regent's first endowed chair. This endowment was an important confirmation of the growing importance of the Cantonese Christian community, which was also reflected in other developments at Regent around this time, including the initiation of a Chinese Studies Programme in 1985. Packer remained Chee Professor until his retirement in 1996, at the age of seventy.

While Packer's reputation as a classic Reformed theologian in the tradition of the Puritans was a significant draw to a large constituency, his interest in spirituality was valued by many others. Packer frequently teamed up with James Houston, and subsequently also with Eugene Peterson following his appointment to the James M. Houston Chair of Spiritual theology from 1993 to 1998, to run seminars and classes on evangelical spirituality, concentrating on the issue of retrieving past resources for present-day Christian living.[1] Many clearly saw Regent College as being both innovative and traditional in its approach, while addressing the needs of lay Christians seeking to lead authentically Christian lives in complex and often conflicted situations. As I know from many personal conversations, Regent College summer schools in the 1990s were seen by many lay Christians and pastors as oases of spiritual refreshment, often featuring headlining presentations by Packer, Peterson and Houston.

Packer, however, also developed a significant teaching and ministerial role beyond Regent College, which extended both his and the College's reach. After allowing himself the fall of 1979 and all of 1980 to settle in at Regent, Packer resumed a full speaking schedule. Major lecture series included the Ryan Lectures at Asbury

Theological Seminary in Wilmore, Kentucky (1982); the Staley Lectures at the Lutheran Bible Institute in Seattle (1982); the Day-Higginbotham Lectures at Southwestern Seminary in Fort Worth, Texas (1985); and the Reformation Heritage Lectures at Beeson Divinity School in Birmingham, Alabama (1994). Packer also undertook visits to a large number of divinity schools, including Canadian Theological Seminary in Regina, Saskatoon (1981), Westminster Theological Seminary, Escondido, California (from 1982), Conservative Baptist Seminary in Denver, Colorado (1982) and the Bible Institute of Hawaii (1983). He also served as a visiting professor (generally involving extended or repeat visits) at Reformed Theological Seminary in Jackson, Mississippi (from 1985) and at New College, Berkeley (from 1985).

Although Packer's role was primarily positive and constructive, especially in his teaching at Regent College, he nevertheless became involved in controversies. Some of these reinforced a wider perception that Packer was the gatekeeper of traditional evangelical orthodoxy; some pointed to Packer stretching the envelope of traditional evangelical attitudes and practices in ways that have subsequently become more widely accepted. We have already noted an example of the former – Packer's 1991 essay 'Let's Stop Making Women Presbyters' – which took some by surprise on account of its apparent unwillingness to acknowledge a legitimate diversity of evangelical opinions on this matter in a shifting cultural context. But some would say that a better example lies to hand in Packer's engagement with the growing debate over universalism and conditional immortality within evangelicalism.

The Controversy over Conditional Immortality

Packer's early article 'The Problem of Universalism Today' drew a sharp distinction between two senses of the term 'universalism': the 'universal Christian claim' on humanity, grounded in Jesus Christ as the one and only Saviour, and the universal need for redemption; and as the universal restoration of humanity 'to the fellowship with God for which Adam was made, and from which he fell'.[2] Packer notes that it is the first form of universalism which establishes the credentials of Christianity as a world religion and gives a solid intellectual foundation to its missionary outlook; the second, however, threatens to erode the distinctiveness, authenticity and integrity of the Christian faith, and rob it of its evangelistic thrust.

Yet the debate intensified and moved to somewhat different questions in 1988, when two leading conservative evangelicals – John Stott and Philip E. Hughes, a former librarian of Latimer House – published works setting out their hitherto private doubts concerning the traditional understanding of the nature of hell and eternal punishment, and tentatively advocated annihilationism as a serious option for evangelicals.[3] Hughes served as Professor of Theology at Westminster Theological Seminary, and was one of the editors of *Westminster Theological Journal* – positions which placed him at the heart of conservative evangelical orthodoxy in the United States.

Stott made it clear that he stated his views with some hesitation, partly on account of his 'great respect for longstanding tradition which claims to be a true interpretation of Scripture' and partly because of his high regard and concern for 'the unity of the worldwide evangelical constituency'.[4] The veteran English conservative evangelical John Wenham, who had been Vice-Principal during Packer's first period at Tyndale Hall, Bristol, then declared that he had privately come round to this way of thinking as early as 1934, partly through the influence of Basil Atkinson, widely regarded as a bastion of orthodoxy in evangelical student circles.[5] As early as 1973, Wenham had publicly stated that evangelicals should consider themselves as being 'under no obligation to defend the notion of unending torment until the arguments of the conditionalists have been refuted'.[6]

Hughes, Stott and Wenham were former colleagues of Packer, with whom he had worked closely in the past, especially in connection with Latimer House. It was not an easy situation for Packer, in that his personal regard for the people concerned had to be set against his fundamental belief that their ideas were wrong. Packer responded to these developments in the annual Leon Morris Lecture, delivered to the Evangelical Alliance in the Australian city of

Melbourne on Friday, 31 August 1990, which dealt with 'The Problem of Eternal Punishment'.[7]

The lecture is interesting in many ways, not least because it implicitly raises the question of whether evangelicalism is to be defined primarily by a love of the Bible, and a determination to set it at the heart of Christian thinking and living, or additionally or alternatively by certain specific intellectual outcomes of reflection on the Bible. To put this another way, is an evangelical committed to particular interpretations of the Bible, rather than to simply making the Bible the starting point and ultimate judge of all doctrinal affirmations? If evangelicals regard no human authority as standing above the Bible, how can the reliability of various competing interpretations of the Bible be judged without placing a human authority – such as a committee or influential preacher – above that of the Bible?[8]

Such questions were addressed at a consultation co-sponsored by the National Association of Evangelicals and Trinity Evangelical Divinity School in May 1989, during which Packer spoke on these issues, setting out essentially the same points he would make a year later in Melbourne. In responding to Packer's article, John Ankerberg and John Weldon argued that believing in eternal punishment was a litmus test which showed up whether someone was an evangelical or not: 'The doctrine of eternal punishment is the watershed between evangelical and non-evangelical thought.'[9] Packer was here cited as a touchstone for authentic evangelical beliefs.

Yet it was not long before Packer was accused of being thoroughly unevangelical by many of those who had cited and commended him with such approval. The cause of this opprobrium was Packer's involvement in 'Evangelicals and Catholics Together'.

The Controversy over Evangelical Collaboration with Catholicism

During the 1990s, a group of senior evangelicals in North America came to the conclusion that they ought to begin discussions about possible limited cooperation with individual senior Roman Catholics. The election of Bill Clinton as the forty-second President of the

United States in 1992 was seen by many Americans as marking the rise of secularism and hostility towards Christianity in the public arena. Although this perception is now generally regarded as having been misplaced, the threat seemed real enough at the time. It persuaded some senior evangelical Protestants and Catholics that they had some serious talking to do. Packer was in the forefront of these discussions.

Why? It might at first seem deeply implausible that a leading evangelical theologian, steeped in the heritage of the Protestant Reformation of the sixteenth century, should commend conversations and potential collaboration with Catholicism. But Packer was convinced that his experience of working with Anglo-Catholic critics of liberalism in England could be transposed to North America. There was no question of evangelicals abandoning the Reformation or endorsing Catholicism. For Packer, a rising tide of secularism mandated dialogue and collaboration between individual evangelicals and individual Catholics on how to engage and counter such developments, while at the same time acknowledging the differences between them.

Two books helped to create this impression of a potentially beleaguered Christianity in North America and offered assessments of possible ways ahead. Richard John Neuhaus's *Naked Public Square* (1984) was widely acclaimed as a study that demonstrated the way in which religion was being systematically eliminated from the public life of the United States. Neuhaus, a Lutheran who had become a Catholic, stressed the need for a Christian witness in this 'naked public square' of American public life. The book was widely welcomed by committed Christians across a range of denominations. The debate was taken further by Charles Colson's *Kingdoms in Conflict* (1987). Colson, a Reagan White House staffer who was converted to evangelical Christianity in the aftermath of the Watergate scandal, sounded a similar note, which was developed still further in his *The Body: Being Light in Darkness* (1992).

Two broad potential strategies emerged within North American evangelicalism during the 1990s in response to the perception that American culture was moving into new and uncharted territories, characterised by an increasingly secular outlook. Catholicism might be an ally in such a struggle. But could an alliance of this kind be sustained without theological compromise and the dilution of evangelical identity? What about the Reformation heritage, which remained important, if not defining, for many within the American evangelical movement?

The first strategy envisaged evangelicals resolving to have nothing to do with Roman Catholics on account of the continuing doctrinal disagreements associated with the agenda of the Reformation. This approach had the merit of the total maintenance of doctrinal integrity. For many evangelicals of the early 1990s, Roman Catholicism was to be seen as a deformed version of Christianity, if it could be described as Christianity at all. Yet this seemed to rule out collaboration with others in the face of a rising tide of secularism.

A second possible strategy involved evangelicals collaborating with Roman Catholics on a limited range of issues, while allowing that crucial differences remained on others. This approach maintained doctrinal integrity by means of an explicit acknowledgement that disagreements remain, while at the same time permitting collaboration on a series of moral, social and political issues, and the mutual defence of Christian orthodoxy against secularism, liberalism and non-Christian religions. Yet it left unresolved the question of how the core doctrinal disagreements of the sixteenth-century Reformation were to be handled. Could they just be ignored? Or understated for pragmatic reasons?   *NO - PMW - 2022*

The document 'Evangelicals and Catholics Together' represents a manifesto for the second of the two approaches just outlined. The document was issued in March 1994, and built on the work of Colson and Neuhaus, who had gradually brought together a network group of individual evangelicals and Catholics who were sympathetic to the idea of collaborative witness in the public arena. The network was never intended to represent denominations or denominational concerns, but was envisaged as a working group exploring the ways in which individual Christians might work together in the face of what appeared to be an increasingly hostile public arena. This was a distinctively American discussion; evangelicals in Britain, embedded in a somewhat different cultural context, did not experience the sense of secular encroachment or a threat of overt secularisation of the public arena to the same extent.

A number of leading evangelicals publicly endorsed the 'Evangelicals and Catholics Together' statement, including William Abraham (Perkins School of Theology), Os Guinness (Trinity Forum), Richard Mouw (Fuller Theological Seminary), Mark Noll (Wheaton College), Thomas Oden (Drew University), Pat Robertson (Regent University) – and Packer himself. In many ways, Packer here adopted the same basic principles in dealing with Catholicism in 1994 as he had in his earlier dealings with Anglo-Catholicism within the Church of England around 1970 (see p. 94). This was not a new development in Packer's thinking, but the extension of an existing understanding of the manner in which evangelicals should relate to other Christians. It represents an excellent example of what Packer termed 'grassroots co-belligerence'. As he would put it, the 'Evangelicals and Catholics Together' document 'identifies common enemies (unbelief, sin, cultural apostasy) and pleads that the Christian counterattack on these things be cooperative up to the limit of what divergent convictions allow'.[10]

From Packer's perspective, the statement built a platform on which evangelicals and Catholics who shared a common faith in the Trinity, the incarnation, the atonement and new birth could unite and work together in reaching out to an increasingly secular society. In this context, Packer reaffirmed the words of C. S. Lewis: 'When all is said (and truly said) about the divisions of Christendom, there remains, by God's mercy, an enormous common ground.'[11] For Packer, it was important to occupy that 'common ground' by seeking substantive convergence on issues of major cultural importance, without forfeiting or fudging any specific historical theological truth-claims. It came as a surprise to him to learn that the document was being read as some kind of mandate for the convergence of churches. For Packer, it seemed quite clear that 'Evangelicals and Catholics Together' was a parachurch document in which individual evangelicals and Catholics agreed to work together for limited yet strategic purposes.[12]

In Packer's view, the present needs of both Church and community in the Western world called out for some such collaboration across denominational divides. Two main considerations prompted this conclusion on his part. First, that the 'slide into secularism and paganism that is so much a mark of current culture' demands that there should be some kind of 'alliance of all who love the Bible and its Christ'. A united Christian witness is necessary in the face of an escalating secular cultural situation. Packer stressed that he is not advocating official collaboration between denominations, but individual alliances across denominational divides, along the lines of the parachurch coalitions already existing within evangelicalism itself.

Second, the historic division between 'relatively homogeneous Protestant churches and a relatively homogeneous Church of Rome' reflects a situation which no longer pertains. A new division has emerged within Christianity, which is of considerably greater importance – the division between theological conservatives (whom Packer prefers to term 'conservationists') who 'honour the Christ of the Bible and historic creeds and confessions' on the one hand, and 'theological liberals and radicals' on the other. This division can be seen within both the Protestant and Catholic Churches. Why should not conservatives form an alliance across their denominations to fight liberalism and radicalism within their denominations, and more broadly? 'Domestic differences about salvation and the Church should not hinder us from joint action in seeking to re-Christianize the North American milieu.' Again, this represents the consistent application of Packer's understanding of 'co-belligerence' which he had worked out within his original English context back in the 1960s (see pp. 93–4).

The document (and particularly Packer's endorsement) gave rise to angry criticisms from many senior American evangelicals, who saw Packer as a traitor to the Protestant and evangelical causes.[13] They argued that Catholics and Protestants were antithetically opposed, with the result that neither could legitimately regard the other as being Christian with any integrity or honesty. Protestants should therefore treat Catholics as non-Christian or anti-Christian (and vice versa). It was a single-shot response, in that once this point had been made, no further discussion was possible. The result was that those who believed that such dialogue was dishonest refused to have anything to do with it, leaving those who disagreed with them to get on with their discussions. The dialogue thus continued, without those who objected to it.

But why limit this approach to collaboration with individual Catholics? What about Orthodoxy, then emerging as a major presence in North America through immigration from Greece and other parts of Eastern Europe? In the spring of 1995, Packer took this strategy a stage further. He was invited to attend the Aiken Conference, organised by Orthodox Christians, which had been convened to test whether an 'ecumenical orthodoxy', solidly based upon the classic Christian faith, can become the foundation for a unified and transformative vision to the modern age. Packer's response to this question was strongly affirmative and developed further his policy of 'collaboration within and across "great-tradition Christianity"'.

Retirement: The 'Last Crusade'

Packer finally retired as the first Sangwoo Yountong Chee Professor of Theology at Regent College in the summer of 1996. His formal retirement did not, however, end his relationship with Regent College. He was appointed to a Board of Governors Professorship of Theology,[14] and continued to play a role in the College's teaching ministry for two further decades, particularly through its summer schools. That same year, the Evangelical Christian Publishers Association awarded him the Jordan Lifetime Achievement Award for his exceptional contribution to the Christian publishing industry. Other awards flowed in throughout his retirement – for example, in 2012 Packer was awarded the Bavinck Prize for Outstanding Reformed Contribution to the Church, the Academy or Public Life. Regent College itself honoured Packer further in 2006 by establishing the 'J. I. Packer Chair in Theology', with the aim of continuing Packer's theological legacy.

For Packer, of course, the word 'retirement' meant little more than disengagement from administrative and formal teaching commitments at Regent College. He continued to remain an active member of the College community, and used his new freedom to accept speaking engagements and writing commitments which he would previously have had difficulty accommodating in his calendar.[15]

Packer continued to act as a theological advisor and contributor to *Christianity Today*, and played a major role in developing and promoting the *English Standard Version*, a new translation of the Bible published in 2001.[16] Packer was a Canadian citizen and continued to reside in Vancouver throughout his retirement.

Yet in his retirement, Packer took on a project which he designated his 'last crusade' – catechetics. As I reflected on Packer's remarkable range of writings and his extensive lectures some years ago, I tried to find a single word that summarised his focus and achievement. I eventually settled on the word 'theologiser', meaning someone who actively does theology, and is concerned with the communication and enactment of Christian ideas. While Packer did not raise any objections to being labelled in this way, he suggested to me that there might be a better description – namely, that he was a 'latter day catechist'. We need to take him seriously when he quipped in 2010 that 'Packer's last crusade' would be a call for the Church to rediscover its lost art of catechesis.

So what led Packer to this conclusion? The word 'catechesis' is unfamiliar to many and is likely to leave some readers baffled. For Packer, however, it designates something that needs to be recovered and respected – that is, the church's ministry of grounding new believers in the rudiments of Christianity. But catechesis is not simply about helping new believers to inhabit the landscape of the Christian faith; it is an act of discipleship on the part of mature believers, leading to the 'growing of God's people in the gospel and its implications for doctrine, devotion, duty, and delight'. Accordingly, the intended outcome of catechesis is therefore a body of 'Christians who know their faith, can explain it to enquirers and sustain it against skeptics, and can put it to work in evangelism, church fellowship, and the many forms of service to God and man for which circumstances call'.[17]

Back in 1977, Packer set out his basic understanding of the importance of catechesis in his work *I Want to be a Christian*.[18] That understanding of its potential forms and structures remains largely unchanged; what has altered is his perception of its importance. It has always been *important*; given cultural changes in the West in the twenty-first century, it is now *vital*. Christians need to be helped to grow into their faith – not moving on *from* the gospel, but rather moving on *within* the gospel.[19]

For Packer, catechesis is essential for a Church that is to survive and prosper in a Western cultural context that sees Christianity as strange, if not alien or hostile. As Packer realised when he wrestled with the Keswick holiness teaching back in the 1940s, 'well-intentioned minds and hearts will repeatedly go off track' unless they are guided and guarded by good theology. The formulation of Christian truth is inseparable from its application in Christian living. For Packer, a failure to catechise can only lead to 'undernourished' Christians, and hence to an emaciated church, which is incapable of witnessing effectively to its faith on the one hand, and enacting that faith on the other.

Packer is someone who knows what he believes, knows why he believes it, and knows what difference it makes to life. A theologian can only too easily become a narrow specialist in limited areas of doctrine; a catechist invites us to discover the 'fulness of God's truth and wisdom', and presents a 'full-scale account of Christian truth as a whole'. Perhaps most theologians were catechists, before the academic professionalism which emerged during the nineteenth century led to the fragmentation of theology, without any attempt to hold its constituent parts together. What we need, Packer suggests, are Christians who can hold this greater vision of the Christian faith together,[20] and enable others to grasp it and grow into it. For this reason, Packer threw himself into the recovery of catechesis in the life of the Church, serving as theological editor to the document *To Be a Christian: An Anglican Catechism*, produced by the Anglican Church in North America (ACNA).

Yet this 'last crusade' is not to be seen as a new development in Packer's thinking, but rather as a specific refocusing of his lifelong quest for a biblically grounded theology that is applied to the life of individual Christians and to that of the Church as a whole. Packer has always recognised the importance of engaging specific contexts and questions; the new situation in which the churches find themselves in Western culture demands a recovery of the rich intellectual content of the gospel, not simply a rekindling of our enthusiasm for its themes.

Conclusion

On Tuesday, 19 July 2016, both Regent College and St John's Church, Vancouver, marked Packer's ninetieth birthday, a few days in advance of the event. It was a happy occasion, with generous tributes to Packer from friends and colleagues, enlivened still further by a jazz band. The highlight of the occasion was the announcement that a special edition of the Regent College journal *Crux* would honour Packer's ongoing contributions to the Church and the academy. In November of that year, Packer's contribution as a theologian, ecumenist and churchman was recognised at the annual meeting of the Evangelical Theological Society in San Antonio, Texas.[21]

By then, however, Packer was in decline. Macular degeneration had already developed in his left eye; over the Christmas season of 2015, it developed also in his right eye and he was no longer able to read or write. This marked the end of a remarkable writing and speaking ministry. Perhaps it was anticipated in some of Packer's final writings, which openly (and often movingly) engaged questions of human weakness and ageing, and how these were to be interpreted theologically.[22]

In those reflections, Packer recalled his former Headmaster at the Crypt School in Gloucester in the early 1940s – David Gwynn Williams, known slightly irreverently as 'Bill' to his students. He had enquired about Williams' health some years earlier, and had been told that he was 'very low'. Having lost any Christian faith, he was simply 'waiting for the end'. Packer saw this loss of hope on the part of his former role model as pointing to one of the most remarkable characteristics of the gospel – its capacity to create and sustain a life of hope. 'If the light of hope goes out, life shrinks to mere existence, something far less than life was meant to be.'[23] For Packer, such a robust hope is the key to living meaningfully in the final stages of life.

I met Packer for the last time in his Vancouver home on the afternoon of Thursday, 20 September 2018. I had been giving a series of lectures at Regent College, which ended that morning. I was due to travel back to London by the late evening flight from Vancouver, so had the afternoon free. Although Packer had been suffering from pneumonia, he was well enough for me to visit him at his home. We spent an enjoyable afternoon reminiscing about Oxford and reflecting on his long period in England, as well as talking theology. His mind was as sharp as ever, his eyes twinkling as he spoke of the great theological themes that had so animated him throughout his career. We hugged each other when the time came for me to leave. I think we both knew we would never see each other again.

Epilogue

The world seemed to slow down in March 2020, as the COVID pandemic swept across the continents. Many national and regional governments restricted the movements and activities of people in a bid to limit the impact of the virus on their fragile healthcare systems. British Columbia, like all other Canadian provinces, called on residents to practise physical distancing and to refrain from travelling. Schools and colleges were shut down. Regent College switched to online delivery of its teaching, including its highly regarded summer school.

By this time, Packer was already virtually housebound. He had been unable to attend the 7.30 a.m. Sunday service at St John's, Vancouver since November, due to his increasing frailty. Friends from Regent College and St John's visited him and Kit regularly, often bringing them meals. Packer had begun to experience falls at home, sometimes resulting in head injuries which at times impaired his ability to speak. Following a particularly serious fall in June, Packer was admitted to Vancouver General Hospital for surgery on his hip, and afterwards was transferred to UBC Hospital to recuperate.

Yet it became clear that Packer was gradually losing strength. On Sunday, 12 July, Packer's doctor told Kit that he probably had only a few more days to live. The next day, he shared in a Communion service with Dan Gifford, vicar of St John's, Vancouver, in a room overlooking Wesbrook Mall, with a clear view of Regent College on the other side of the street. On the morning of Friday, 17 July, Kit arrived to visit Packer, accompanied by Dan Gifford, to mark their sixty-sixth wedding anniversary. They found Packer unconscious. He died peacefully at 11.40 a.m. After leaving the hospital, Kit and Dan walked over the street to Regent. They found Bill Reimer – Regent's legendary bookstore manager – at work in his office, and told him what had happened. Jeff Greenman, President of Regent College, broke the news to the college community an hour later.

Tributes began to pour in. *Christianity Today* posted a series of affectionate assessments of Packer's significance from evangelical thought leaders, along with wider reflections on his legacy. One of the most moving tributes was from James Houston, the founding Principal of Regent College, who originally appointed Packer to the Regent faculty back in the late 1970s. Houston gave the eulogy at the funeral service at St John's, Vancouver on 23 July, speaking of Packer as his 'oldest friend', recalling their days together at Oxford in the late 1940s, and praising his 'extraordinary clarity of mind'.

The COVID emergency measures were still in force, and only fifty invited guests were admitted to the funeral, wearing face masks and maintaining physical distance. No congregational singing was allowed. Yet the gospel message of hope was still affirmed, perhaps most powerfully through the famous words of Paul, which were read by Packer's Regent colleague Craig Gay in the *English Standard Version* translation, which Packer had helped to shape:

> For I am sure that neither death nor life, nor angels nor rulers, nor things present nor things to come, nor powers, nor height nor depth, nor anything else in all creation, will be able to separate us from the love of God in Christ Jesus our Lord (Romans 8:38–9).

So what is Packer's legacy? Time alone will tell, although this short book has mapped out some possibilities. Many found in Packer's writings an intelligent and deep vision of the Christian faith, firmly rooted in the Bible on the one hand, and in the long tradition of biblical reflection, especially within Puritanism, on the other. Others found him to be a gateway to the riches of the believing past, like one who opened up a treasure chest of wisdom and helped us explore what lay within. Yet perhaps his legacy might lie most enduringly in his insistence that we need to go deeper into our faith, not resting content with superficial engagement. We can learn from those who have done this before us, and who urge us to follow them in discovering and exploring what Packer so eloquently called the 'biggest thing that ever was'.

Notes

Chapter 1

1 See his remarkable piece ''Tecs, Thrillers, and Westerns', *Christianity Today*, 8 (November 1985), p. 12.

2 J. I. Packer, *Keep in Step with the Spirit* (Downers Grove, IL: InterVarsity Press, 1984), p. 129.

3 J. I. Packer, 'In Quest of Canonical Interpretation', in Robert K. Johnston, *The Use of the Bible in Theology: Evangelical Opinions* (Atlanta: John Knox Press, 1985), pp. 35–55; quote at p. 39.

4 J. I. Packer, *Puritan Portaits* (Fearn, Ross-shire: Christian Focus, 2012), pp. 79–80.

5 John Pawson, *Sermons* (Leeds: Edward Baines, 1809), pp. 6–7.

6 Michael A. G. Haykin, ' "Dissent Warmed Its Hands at Grimshaw's Fire": William Grimshaw of Haworth and the Baptists of Yorkshire', *Perichoresis*, 7, 1 (2009), pp. 23–37.

7 J. I. Packer, *A Quest for Godliness: The Puritan Vision of the Christian Life* (Wheaton, IL: Crossway Books, 1990), p. 12.

8 J. I. Packer, *A Kind of Noah's Ark? The Anglican Commitment to Comprehensiveness*, Latimer Study No. 10 (Oxford: Latimer House, 1981), p. 2.

Chapter 2

1 C. S. Lewis, 'On the Reading of Old Books', in *Essay Collection: Faith, Christianity and the Church* (London: HarperCollins, 2002), p. 440.

2 J. I. Packer, 'Living Truth for a Dying World: The Message of C. S. Lewis', *Crux*, 34, 4 (1998), pp. 3–12; quote at p. 3.

3 J. I. Packer, 'On from Orr: The Cultural Crisis, Rational Realism, and Incarnational Ontology', *Crux* 32, 3 (1996), pp. 12–26.

4 C. S. Lewis, *An Experiment in Criticism* (Cambridge: Cambridge University Press, 1961), pp. 140–1.
5 Lewis, *An Experiment in Criticism*, p. 139.
6 Anthony C. Thiselton, *The Two Horizons: New Testament Hermeneutics and Philosophical Description with Special Reference to Heidegger, Bultmann, Gadamer, and Wittgenstein* (Exeter: Paternoster, 1980), pp. 15–16.
7 John Stott, *The Contemporary Christian: An Urgent Plea for Double Listening* (Leicester: InterVarsity Press, 1992), p. 13. For Stott's use of *The Two Horizons*, see John Stott, *I Believe in Preaching* (London: Hodder & Stoughton, 1982), pp. 137–8.
8 J. I. Packer, 'Infallible Scripture and the Role of Hermeneutics', in D. A. Carson and J. D. Woodbridge (eds), *Scripture and Truth* (Grand Rapids, MI: Zondervan, 1983), pp. 325–56. Cf. Thiselton, *The Two Horizons*, pp. 303–10.
9 For a good set of essays on this theme, see Darren Sarisky (ed.), *Theologies of Retrieval: An Exploration and Appraisal* (London: Bloomsbury, 2017).

Chapter 3

1 American readers might like to know that 'table tennis' translates as 'ping pong'.
2 J. I. Packer, 'The Puritan Treatment of Justification by Faith', *The Evangelical Quarterly*, 24.3 (1952), pp. 131–43.
3 The BCMS also established a women's college in October 1930 in Cotham Park, Bristol, which was named Dalton House.

Chapter 4

1 Martyn Lloyd-Jones, 'Can We Learn From History?', in J. I. Packer (ed.), *Puritan Papers*, 5, 1968/9 (Phillipsburg, NJ: Presbyterian & Reformed Publishing, 2005), pp. 215–16.
2 Packer, *A Quest for Godliness*, p. 21.
3 Packer, *Puritan Portraits*, p. 23. The list of writers Packer discusses can all be described as 'Puritan' in the popular sense of the term; historians, however, would point out that they hold quite different, even divergent, views on such issues as biblical interpretation, church polity and the sacraments.

4 Packer, *Puritan Portraits*, pp. 23–6.

5 Packer, *A Quest for Godliness*, p. 28.

6 Packer, *A Quest for Godliness*, p. 215.

7 James Henley Thornwell, *Collected Writings*, 4 vols (Richmond, VA: Presbyterian Committee of Publication, 1870–3), vol. 1, p. 34.

8 Packer, *A Quest for Godliness*, p. 12.

9 John Owen, 'Mortification of Sin in Believers', in W. H. Goold (ed.), *The Works of John Owen*, 24 vols (Edinburgh: Banner of Truth, 1967), vol. 6, p. 9.

10 Packer, *A Quest for Godliness*, p. 15.

11 Packer, *A Quest for Godliness*, p. 14.

12 Packer, *A Quest for Godliness*, p. 13.

13 Packer, *A Quest for Godliness*, p. 77.

14 John Piper, *Desiring God: Meditations of a Christian Hedonist* (Sisters, OR: Multnomah Press, 1986).

15 John Piper, 'A Personal Encounter with Jonathan Edwards', *The Reformed Journal*, 28, 11 (1978), pp. 13–17.

Chapter 5

1 J. I. Packer, review of Steven Barabas, *So Great Salvation: The History and Message of the Keswick Convention*, *Evangelical Quarterly* (1955), 27, pp. 153–67.

2 J. I. Packer, ' "Keswick" and the Reformed Doctrine of Sanctification', *Evangelical Quarterly* 2, no.3 (1955), pp. 153–67.

3 Alister Chapman, *Godly Ambition: John Stott and the Evangelical Movement* (Oxford: Oxford University Press, 2012), pp. 43–4.

4 Chapman, *Godly Ambition*, pp. 39–48.

5 A. G. Hebert, *Fundamentalism and the Church of God* (London: SCM Press, 1957).

6 J. I. Packer, *'Fundamentalism' and the Word of God* (Grand Rapids, MI: Eerdmans, 1958), p. 29.

7 Packer, *'Fundamentalism' and the Word of God*, p. 136.

8 Billy Graham, *How to be Born Again* (Dallas, TX: Word, 1977), p. 162.

9 Packer, *A Quest for Godliness*, p. 293.

10 J. I. Packer, 'Puritan Evangelism', *Banner of Truth* (4 February 1957), pp. 4–13.

11 Packer, 'Puritan Evangelism', pp. 4–13.

12 J. I. Packer, 'The Puritan View of Preaching the Gospel' in *How Shall They Hear: A Symposium* (London: Evangelical Magazine, 1960), pp. 11–21.

13 J. I. Packer, *Evangelism and the Sovereignty of God* (Downers Grove, IL: InterVarsity Press, 2012), p. 35.

14 Packer, *Evangelism and the Sovereignty of God*, p. 18.

15 Packer, *Evangelism and the Sovereignty of God*, p. 23.

16 Packer, *Evangelism and the Sovereignty of God*, p. 21.

17 Packer, *Evangelism and the Sovereignty of God*, pp. 34–5.

18 Packer, *Evangelism and the Sovereignty of God*, p. 99.

Chapter 6

1 Alister E. McGrath (ed.), *The NIV Thematic Study Bible* (London: Hodder & Stoughton, 1998).

2 For Packer's involvement in this project, see Leland Ryken, *J. I. Packer: An Evangelical Life* (Wheaton, IL: Crossway Books, 2015), pp. 258–62.

3 'J. I. Packer: A Balanced Bible Study Diet', *Bible Study Magazine* (Nov–Dec 2009).

4 J. I. Packer, 'Reading the Bible Theologically', in *English Standard Version Study Bible* (Wheaton, IL: Crossway Books, 2008), pp. 2567.

5 J. I. Packer, 'Revelation and Inspiration', in Francis Davidson, Ernest F. Kevan and Alan M. Stibbs (eds), *The New Bible Commentary* (London: Inter-Varsity Fellowship, 1954), pp. 12–18.

6 For an excellent example of this kind of approach, see Vaughan Roberts, *God's Big Picture: Tracing the Storyline of the Bible* (Downers Grove, IL: InterVarsity Press, 2002).

7 See, for example, Packer, 'Hermeneutics and Biblical Authority', *The Churchman*, 81 (1967), pp. 3–12.

8 J. I. Packer, 'Evangelical Foundations for Spirituality', in Marcus Bockmuehl and Helmut Burkhardt (eds), *Gott Lieben und seine Gebote halten: In memoriam Klaus Bockmuehl* (Basel: Brunner Verlag, 1991), pp. 149–62.

9 J. I. Packer, 'In Quest of Canonical Interpretation', in Robert K. Johnston, *The Use of the Bible in Theology: Evangelical Opinions* (Atlanta: John Knox Press, 1985), p. 47.

10 Packer, 'In Quest of Canonical Interpretation', p. 45.

11 Packer, 'In Quest of Canonical Interpretation', p. 47.

12 Packer, 'In Quest of Canonical Interpretation', p. 53.

13 Packer, 'Reading the Bible Theologically', p. 2567.

14 J. I. Packer, *Concise Theology: A Guide to Historic Christian Beliefs* (Wheaton, IL: Tyndale House, 1993), pp. 134–5.

15 J. I. Packer, *Beyond the Battle for the Bible* (Westchester, IL: Cornerstone Books, 1980), pp. 144–5.

16 Packer, 'In Quest of Canonical Interpretation', p. 48.

17 J. I. Packer, 'The Comfort of Conservatism', in Michael Horton (ed.), *Power Religion* (Chicago: Moody, 1992), pp. 283–99.

Chapter 7

1 John Stott, *Basic Christianity* (London: Inter-Varsity Fellowship, 1958), p. 7.

2 Chapman, *Godly Ambition: John Stott and the Evangelical Movement*, pp. 53–77.

3 J. I. Packer, 'A Strategic Priority' (unpublished memorandum, December 1958), p. 1.

4 For background, see Eric James, *A Life of Bishop John A. T. Robinson* (London: Collins, 1987). For an analysis of the reaction, see David L. Edwards (ed.), *The Honest to God Debate: Some Reactions to the Book 'Honest to God'* (London: SCM Press, 1963).

5 J. I. Packer, *Keep Yourselves from Idols: A Discussion of 'Honest to God' by John A. T. Robinson* (London: Church Book Room Press, 1963).

6 John A. T. Robinson, *Honest to God* (London: SCM Press, 1963), p. 67.

7 Packer, *Keep Yourselves from Idols*, p. 5.

8 Robinson, *Honest to God*, p. 7.

9 Robinson, *Honest to God*, p. 114.

10 Packer, *Keep Yourselves from Idols*, p. 17.

11 Packer, *Keep Yourselves from Idols*, p. 17.

12 Cited in Edwards (ed.), *The Honest to God Debate*, p. 93.

13 For the complexities underlying the situation, and the difficulties in describing the various forms of evangelicalism which were regnant at that time, see the excellent collection of papers assembled in Andrew Atherstone and John G. Maiden (eds), *Evangelicalism and the Church of England in the Twentieth Century* (Woodbridge, Suffolk: Boydell Press, 2014).

14 For a good account, see Diarmaid MacCulloch, *Thomas Cranmer: A Life* (New Haven, CT: Yale University Press, 1996).

15 J. I. Packer and R. T. Beckwith, *The Thirty-Nine Articles: Their Place and Use Today* (Oxford: Latimer House, 1984), pp. 51–2.

16 J. I. Packer, *The Thirty-Nine Articles* (London: Church Pastoral Aid Society, 1961).

17 Oliver O'Donovan, *On the Thirty-Nine Articles: A Conversation with Tudor Christianity* (Exeter: Paternoster Press, 1986), p.115.

18 For a good example of this approach at the time, see Geoffrey W. Bromiley, 'The Purpose and Function of the Thirty-Nine Articles', *The Churchman*, 73, 2 (1959), pp. 60–5.

19 Alister Chapman, 'Secularisation and the Ministry of John R. W. Stott at All Souls, Langham Place, 1950–1970', *Journal of Ecclesiastical History*, 56 (2005), pp. 496–513. See also Alister Chapman, 'The International Context of Secularization in England: The End of Empire, Immigration, and the Decline of Christian National Identity, 1945–1970', *Journal of British Studies* (2015), pp. 163–89.

20 Peter Webster, *Archbishop Ramsey: The Shape of the Church* (Farnham: Ashgate, 2015), p. 47.

21 For an account, see Iain H. Murray, *D. Martyn Lloyd-Jones: The Fight of Faith, 1939–1981* (Edinburgh: Banner of Truth, 1990), pp. 501–6.

22 Details with primary sources in Murray, *Lloyd-Jones*, pp. 528–32.

23 The 'Statement of Principles' is reprinted in Murray, *Lloyd-Jones*, pp. 536–7. Note especially the fifth principle ('Those who are at present in denominations linked with the World Council of Churches are agreed that separation from such denominations is inevitable').

24 J. I. Packer, *The Evangelical Anglican Identity Problem: An Analysis*, Latimer Study No. 1 (Oxford: Latimer House, 1978); Packer, *A Kind of Noah's Ark?* For Packer's earlier views on the nature of the Church, see J. I. Packer, 'The Nature of the Church', in C. F. H. Henry (ed.), *Basic Christian Doctrines* (New York: Rinehard & Winston, 1962), pp. 214–17.

25 Packer, *A Kind of Noah's Ark?*, p. 10.

26 Packer, *A Kind of Noah's Ark?*, p. 36.

27 A report on this conference was presented at the Latimer House Council meeting on 31 March 1966.

28 'Latimer House Study Groups General Report No. 1', November 1967.

29 For some helpful reflections, see Andrew Atherstone, 'The Keele Congress of 1967: A Paradigm Shift in Anglican Evangelical Attitudes', *Journal of Anglican Studies*, 9, 2 (2011), pp. 175–97.

30 'Face to Face with Dr J. I. Packer', *Tyndale Hall Topic* (1967), pp. 1–4; relevant material at p. 4.

31 Jim Packer to Colin Brown, 12 February 1969.

32 Letter to J. Stafford Wright, 30 October 1968.

33 'Face to Face with Dr J. I. Packer', p. 4.

34 See Colin Buchanan, *St John's College Nottingham: From Northwood to Nottingham* (Nottingham: St John's College, 2013).

35 Green and Packer would, however, serve together later as members of the faculty of Regent College, Vancouver, from 1987 to 1992.

36 Three names were suggested by Council members, and it was agreed that they would be invited to the next meeting to be held at All Souls, Langham Place, London on 22 October. In December, the position was finally offered to John Wenham.

Chapter 8

1 For details, see Alister E. McGrath, *Thomas F. Torrance: An Intellectual Biography* (Edinburgh: T. & T. Clark, 1999).

2 As examples of such works, I particularly note 'What did the Cross Achieve? The Logic of Penal Substitution', *Tyndale Bulletin*, 25 (1974), pp. 3–45; and 'On from Orr: The Cultural Crisis, Rational Realism, and Incarnational Ontology', *Crux*, 32, 3 (1996), pp. 12–26.

3 Kate Crehan, *Gramsci's Common Sense: Inequality and its Narratives* (Durham, NC: Duke University Press, 2016), pp. 3–41.

4 See, for example, the substantial study of Glenn T. Miller, *Piety and Intellect: The Aims and Purposes of Ante-Bellum Theological Education* (Atlanta: Scholars Press, 1990).

5 Edward Farley, *Theologia: The Fragmentation and Unity of Theological Education* (Philadelphia: Fortress Press, 1983), pp. x, 7. Farley returned to develop this theme five years later: *The Fragility of Knowledge: Theological Education in the Church and University* (Philadelphia: Fortress Press, 1988).

6 See especially his later articles 'An Introduction to Systematic Spirituality', *Crux*, 26, 1 (1990), pp. 2–8; and 'Evangelical Foundations for Spirituality', pp. 149–62.

7 For an excellent critical study, see Donald J. Payne, *The Theology of the Christian Life in J. I. Packer's Thought: Theological Anthropology, Theological Method, and the Doctrine of Sanctification* (Eugene, OR: Wipf & Stock, 2006). As Payne notes (p. 11), Packer tends to use the terms 'piety', 'spirituality', 'holiness' and 'godliness' interchangeably.

8 I here draw on Packer's articles 'An Introduction to Systematic Spirituality' and 'Evangelical Foundations for Spirituality', which both offer a lucid account of his concept of theology.

9 Packer, 'An Introduction to Systematic Spirituality'.
10 Packer, 'Evangelical Foundations for Spirituality'.
11 Packer, *Puritan Portraits*, p. 81.
12 Packer, 'Evangelical Foundations for Spirituality'.
13 Packer's analysis does not answer all the questions that might be raised at this point. See, for example, the concerns put forward by Payne, *The Theology of the Christian Life in J. I. Packer's Thought*.
14 J. I. Packer, 'The Nature of the Church', p. 217.
15 Packer, 'Evangelical Foundations for Spirituality'.
16 Packer, *Concise Theology*, pp. 35−7.
17 Packer, 'On from Orr.'
18 James Orr, *The Christian View of God and the World as Centring in the Incarnation* (Edinburgh: Andrew Elliot, 1893) pp. 263−4.

Chapter 9

1 I document these complex developments in detail in A. McGrath, *To Know and Serve God: A Biography of James I. Packer* (London: Hodder & Stoughton, 1998).
2 Richard James to Alec Moyter, 26 October 1969.
3 Leslie Paul, *The Deployment and Payment of the Clergy: A Report* (London: Church Information Office, 1964).
4 See further Andrew Atherstone, 'Rescued from the Brink: The Collapse and Resurgence of Wycliffe Hall, Oxford', *Studies in Church History*, 44 (2008), pp. 354−64.
5 For detailed documentation of these complex developments, see McGrath, *To Know and Serve God*.

Chapter 10

1 Chapman, *Godly Ambition*, pp. 85−6.
2 Edward England, *An Unfading Vision: The Adventure of Books* (London: Hodder & Stoughton, 1982) pp. 152−3.
3 Packer, 'An Introduction to Systematic Spirituality', pp. 2−8.
4 Packer, 'An Introduction to Systematic Spirituality', p. 6.
5 J. I. Packer, 'On Knowing God', *Tenth: An Evangelical Quarterly* (July 1975), pp. 11−25.

6 'Pellucid' comes from the Latin verb *perlucere* – to shine through or to allow something to be clearly seen.

7 J. I. Packer, *Knowing God* (London: Hodder & Stoughton, 1975), p. 45.

8 See Mary Morrissey, 'Scripture, Style and Persuasion in Seventeenth-Century English Theories of Preaching', *Journal of Ecclesiastical History*, 53, 4 (2002), pp. 686–706.

9 John Henry Newman, *The Idea of a University* (London: Longmans, Green, & Co, 1852), p. 224.

10 Packer, *Knowing God*, p. 7.

11 John A. Mackay, *A Preface to Christian Theology* (London: Nisbet, 1941), pp. 29–54. For my own use of Mackay's approach, see Alister McGrath, *The Landscape of Faith: An Explorer's Guide to the Christian Faith* (London: SPCK, 2018), pp. 42–4.

12 William Leathem, 'Renewing the Local Church', in J. I. Packer (ed.), *Guidelines: Anglican Evangelicals Face the Future* (London: Falcon, 1967.), pp. 183–209; quote at pp. 198–9.

13 Packer, *Knowing God*, pp. 7–8.

14 See, for example, the overwhelmingly rationalist approach in John Woodhouse, 'Experiencing Confusion', *The Briefing*, 18 February 1992.

15 Packer, *Knowing God*, p. 42.

16 Packer, *Knowing God*, p. 43.

Chapter 11

1 Packer, 'What did the Cross achieve? The Logic of Penal Substitution', pp. 3–45.

2 Citation from photocopied handout for lecture 12, 'Notes on Biblical Inerrancy'.

3 J. I. Packer, 'Battling for the Bible', *Regent College Bulletin*, 9, 4 (Fall, 1979).

4 P. E. Hughes, 'Editorial', *The Churchman*, 76 (1962): pp. 131–5. This editorial was reprinted in pamphlet form and is estimated to have sold some 39,000 copies.

5 The four were John Collins, Michael Harper, David MacInnes and David Watson – each of whom would become a major figure in the English charismatic movement as it subsequently developed.

6 See Packer's early article: J. I. Packer, 'The Holy Spirit and the Local Congregation', *The Churchman*, 78 (1964), pp. 98–108.

7 Packer's important work *Keep in Step with the Spirit* (Downers Grove, IL: InterVarsity Press, 1984) can be seen as a 'coming-of-age gift' to the charismatic movement, both as a mark of appreciation and a suggestion for future reflection.

8 Chapman, *Godly Ambition*, pp. 101–3.

9 The Committee consisted of John Stott (Chairman); David Gillett (Secretary); Garth Grinham, Don Irving, Gavin Reid, Michael Saward and Raymond Turvey.

10 J. I. Packer, 'Jesus Christ the Lord', in J. R. W. Stott (ed.), *Obeying Christ in a Changing World* (London: Collins, 1977), pp. 32–60.

11 Packer, *The Evangelical Identity Problem*.

12 Teddy Saunders and Hugh Sansom, *David Watson: A Biography* (London: Hodder & Stoughton, 1992), p. 186.

13 *The Nottingham Statement* (London: Falcon, 1977), p. 13.

14 Prominent among these were F. F. Bruce, E. Marshall Sheppard, James M. Houston, Ward Gasque and Carl E. Armerding.

15 For two important accounts of the background to Regent College, see Kenneth V. Botton, 'Regent College: An Experiment in Theological Education', PhD thesis, Trinity Evangelical Divinity School, 2004; Charles E. Cotherman, 'Awakening the Lay Evangelical Mind: Francis Schaeffer, James Houston, and the Christian Study Center Movement in North America', PhD Thesis, University of Virginia, 2017, especially pp. 102–53. My own research on the oral history of the College suggests that there are divergent accounts of both the origin and precise focus of its vision.

Chapter 12

1 Roger Scruton, *Conservatism: An Invitation to the Great Tradition* (New York: St Martin's Press, 2017), p. 127.

2 Jaroslav Pelikan, *The Vindication of Tradition* (New Haven, CT: Yale University Press, 1984), p. 65.

3 Packer, 'The Comfort of Conservatism', pp. 283–99.

4 Packer, 'The Comfort of Conservatism', pp. 284–5.

5 Packer, 'The Comfort of Conservatism', p. 289.

6 Packer, 'The Comfort of Conservatism', p. 293.

7 Packer, 'The Comfort of Conservatism', pp. 288–9.

8 See further Stephen R. Holmes, *Listening to the Past: The Place of Tradition*

in Theology (Grand Rapids, MI: Baker Academic, 2002); Daniel H. Williams, *Evangelicals and Tradition: The Formative Influence of the Early Church* (Grand Rapids, MI: Baker Academic, 2005).

9 Packer, *'Fundamentalism' and the Word of God*, p. 48.

10 J. I. Packer, *Truth & Power: The Place of Scripture in the Christian Life* (Downers Grove, IL: InterVarsity Press, 1999), p. 110.

11 Packer, *Truth & Power*, pp. 116–18. See also Packer, 'Comfort of Conservatism', pp. 291–2.

12 For a similar argument, see Robert Wilken, 'The Durability of Orthodoxy', *Word and World*, 2 (1988), pp. 124–32.

13 For the details, see J. I. Packer, 'Why I Walked: Sometimes Loving a Denomination Requires You to Fight', *Christianity Today*, 1 January 2003.

14 J. I. Packer, 'Let's Stop Making Women Presbyters', *Christianity Today*, 11 February 1991. By 'presbyter' Packer means 'the person or persons (usually professional clergy) officially charged with the oversight of a local congregation'.

15 See, for example, Grace Ying May and Hyunhye Pokrifka Joe, 'A Response to J. I. Packer's Position on Women's Ordination', *Priscilla Papers*, 11, 1 (1997), pp. 1–10.

16 Russell Kirk, *The Conservative Mind: From Burke to Eliot*, 3rd revised edn (Chicago: Regnery, 1960).

17 Scruton, *Conservatism*, pp. 127–55, especially pp. 143–4.

18 Henry Mintzberg, Bruce Ahlstrand and Joseph Lampel, *Strategy Safari: A Guided Tour Through the Wilds of Strategic Management* (New York: Free Press, 1998), p. 8.

Chapter 13

1 See Chris Armstrong, 'The Rise, Frustration, and Revival of Evangelical Spiritual Ressourcement', *Journal of Spiritual Formation and Soul Care*, 2, 1 (2009), pp. 113–21.

2 J. I. Parker, 'The Problem of Universalism Today', *Theolog. Review: Australian Journal of the Theological Students Fellowship*, 5/3 (November, 1969), pp. 16–24.

3 Philip E. Hughes, *The True Image: The Origin and Destiny of Man in Christ* (Grand Rapids, MI: Eerdmans, 1988).

4 David L. Edwards with John R. W. Stott, *Essentials* (London: Hodder & Stoughton, 1988), pp. 312–39; quote at p. 319. Stott later clarified his

position, indicating that although he is inclined towards annihilationism, he ultimately remains agnostic on the issue.

5 John Wenham, *Facing Hell: The Story of a Nobody. An Autobiography 1913–1996* (Carlisle: Paternoster Press, 1998), pp. 229–57.

6 J. W. Wenham, *The Goodness of God* (London: InterVarsity Press, 1974), p. 41.

7 J. I. Packer, *The Problem of Eternal Punishment*, Leon Morris Lecture, 1990 (Camberwell: Evangelical Alliance (Victoria), Inc., 1990).

8 I explore this question myself in Alister E. McGrath, *Christianity's Dangerous Idea: The Protestant Revolution* (San Franciso: HarperOne, 2007), pp. 199–213.

9 John Ankerberg and John Weldon, 'Response to J. I. Packer', in Kenneth S. Kantzer and Carl F. H. Henry, *Evangelical Affirmations* (Grand Rapids, MI: Zondervan, 1990), pp. 137–48.

10 J. I. Packer, 'Crosscurrents among Evangelicals', in Charles Colson and Richard J. Neuhaus (eds), *Evangelicals and Catholics Together: Toward a Common Mission* (Dallas: Word, 1995), pp. 147–74. See also Packer's important essay 'Why I Signed It', *Christianity Today*, 12 December 1994, pp. 34–7.

11 C. S. Lewis, *Christian Reflections* (London: Bles, 1967), p. vii.

12 Richard Land and Larry Lewis withdrew their signatures to the statement in April 1995, following concern that their action had unintentionally created the impression that the Southern Baptist Convention had officially endorsed the document. At this stage, Land was serving on the Christian Life Commission of the Convention and Lewis was on its Home Mission Board. Both indicated their continuing personal endorsement of the document.

13 See the trenchant criticism (particularly directed against Packer) in R. C. Sproul, *Faith Alone: The Evangelical Doctrine of Justification* (Grand Rapids, MI: Baker Books, 1995), pp. 183–92. The 'Alliance of Confessing Evangelicals', founded in April 1996, reflected similar concerns. See James Montgomery Boice and Benjamin E. Sasse, *Here We Stand: A Call from Confessing Evangelicals* (Grand Rapids, MI: Baker Books, 1996).

14 Packer and James Houston were honoured with the title of 'Board of Governors Professor' on their respective retirements, rather than the more customary title of 'Professor Emeritus'.

15 The best source for Packer's activities from 1996 onwards is Ryken, *J. I. Packer*.

16 For Packer's involvement in this project, see Ryken, *J. I. Packer*, pp. 258–62.

17 J. I. Packer, *Taking God Seriously: Vital Things We Need to Know* (Wheaton, IL: Crossway Books, 2013), p. 11.

18 J. I. Packer, *I Want to be a Christian* (Eastbourne: Kingsway Publications, 1977).

19 See here Joel Scandrett, '"To Be a Christian": J. I. Packer and the Renewal of Evangelical Catechesis', *Crux*, 52, 1 (2016), pp. 4–12.

20 J. I. Packer and Gary A. Parrett, 'The Lost Art of Catechesis', *Christianity Today*, 12 March 2010. For a fuller treatment of the theme, see J. I. Packer and Gary A. Parrett, *Grounded in the Gospel: Building Believers the Old-Fashioned Way* (Grand Rapids, MI: Baker Books, 2010).

21 For my own contribution to that event, see Alister McGrath, *Mere Discipleship: On Growing in Wisdom and Hope* (London: SPCK, 2018), pp. 112–20.

22 J. I. Packer, *Weakness Is the Way: Life with Christ Our Strength* (Wheaton, IL: Crossway Books, 2013); and *Finishing Our Course with Joy: Guidance from God for Engaging with Our Aging* (Wheaton, IL: Crossway Books, 2014).

23 Packer, *Weakness Is the Way*, pp. 89–90. This work takes the form of a series of meditations on 2 Corinthians. Packer refers to Williams simply as 'Bill' in this discussion.

Further Reading

Biographies of Packer

McGrath, Alister E., *To Know and Serve God: A Biography of James I. Packer* (London: Hodder & Stoughton, 1998); US edition: *J. I. Packer: A Biography* (Grand Rapids, MI: Baker Books , 1998).

Ryken, Leland, *J. I. Packer: An Evangelical Life* (Wheaton, IL: Crossway Books, 2015).

Studies of Packer

George, Timothy (ed.), *J. I. Packer and the Evangelical Future: The Impact of His Life and Thought* (Grand Rapids, MI: Baker Books, 2009).

Lewis, Donald M. and Alister E. McGrath (eds), *Doing Theology for the People of God: Studies in Honor of J. I. Packer* (Downers Grove, IL: InterVarsity Press, 1996).

Payne, Donald J., *The Theology of the Christian Life in J. I. Packer's Thought: Theological Anthropology, Theological Method, and the Doctrine of Sanctification* (Eugene, OR: Wipf & Stock, 2006).

Steer, Roger, *Guarding the Holy Fire: The Evangelicalism of John R. W. Stott, J. I. Packer, and Alister McGrath* (Grand Rapids, MI: Baker Books, 1999).

Storms, C. Samuel, *Packer on the Christian Life: Knowing God in Christ, Walking by the Spirit* (Wheaton, IL: Crossway Books, 2015).

Core Works by J. I. Packer

The best source for a full list of Packer's works up to 2008 is Timothy George (ed.), *J. I. Packer and the Evangelical Future: The Impact of His Life and Thought* (Grand Rapids, MI: Baker Books, 2009), pp. 187–230. For a representative collection of his more important articles, see Alister E. McGrath (ed.), *The J. I. Packer Collection* (Leicester: InterVarsity Press, 1999).

Four major works of representative importance should be noted:

Packer, J. I., *Concise Theology: A Guide to Historic Christian Beliefs* (Wheaton, IL: Tyndale House, 1993).

Packer, J. I., *'Fundamentalism' and the Word of God* (Grand Rapids, MI: Eerdmans, 1958).

Packer, J. I., *Knowing God* (London: Hodder & Stoughton, 1973).

Packer, J. I., *A Quest for Godliness: The Puritan Vision of the Christian Life* (Wheaton, IL: Crossway Books, 1990).

Index

8-17-22
wed.

Also Available from IVP

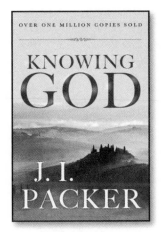

Knowing God
978-0-8308-1651-4

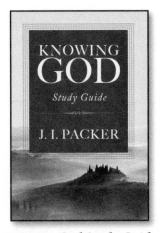

Knowing God Study Guide
978-0-8308-1649-1

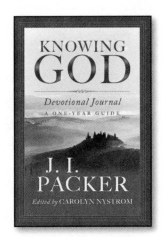

*Knowing God
Devotional Journal*
978-0-8308-3739-7